*Phenomenal Women:
That's Us!*

OTHER TITLES FROM NEW FALCON PUBLICATIONS

Insights
Power Up for Success
The Psychology of Synergy
    By Dr. Madeleine Singer
Cosmic Trigger: Final Secret of the Illuminati
Prometheus Rising
    By Robert Anton Wilson
Undoing Yourself With Energized Meditation
The Pyschopath's Bible
    By Christopher S. Hyatt, Ph.D.
Gems From the Equinox
The Pathworkings of Aleister Crowley
    By Aleister Crowley
Info-Psychology
    By Timothy Leary, Ph.D.
Condensed Chaos: An Introduction to Chaos Magick
    By Phil Hine
PsyberMagick
    By Peter Carroll
Buddhism and Jungian Psychology
    By J. Marvin Spiegelman, Ph.D.
Soul Magic: Understanding Your Journey
    By Katherine Torres, Ph.D.
A Mother Looks At the Gay Child
    By Jesse Davis
Bio-Etheric Healing: A Breakthrough in Alternate Therapies
    By Trudy Lanitis
Conversations With My Dark Side
    By Shanti Ananda
Changing Ourselves, Changing the World
    By Gary Reiss
A Soul's Journey: Whispers From the Light
    By Patricia Idol

And to get your free catalog of *all* of our titles, write to:
New Falcon Publications (Catalog Dept.)
PMB 277
1739 East Broadway Road #1
Tempe, Arizona 85282 U.S.A
And visit our website at **http://www.newfalcon.com**

Phenomenal Women: That's Us!

A Book of Power, Personal Strength, Inner Beauty and Radiant Happiness for Midlife Women

by

Dr. Madeleine Singer

NEW FALCON PUBLICATIONS
TEMPE, ARIZONA, U.S.A.

Copyright © 2000 by Dr. Madeleine Singer

All rights reserved. No part of this book, in part or in whole, may be reproduced, transmitted, or utilized, in any form or by any means, electronic or mechanical, including photocopying, recording, or by any information storage and retrieval system, without permission in writing from the publisher, except for brief quotations in critical articles, books and reviews.

International Standard Book Number: 1-56184-145-5
Library of Congress Catalog Card Number: 99-67450

First Edition 2000

Edited by Martin Ducheny
Cover Art by Béla Kalman

The paper used in this publication meets the minimum requirements of the American National Standard for Permanence of Paper for Printed Library Materials Z39.48-1984

Address all inquiries to:
NEW FALCON PUBLICATIONS
PMB 277
1739 East Broadway Road #1
Tempe, AZ 85282 U.S.A.
(or)
PMB 286
320 East Charleston Blvd. #204
Las Vegas, NV 89104 U.S.A.
website: http://www.newfalcon.com
email: info@newfalcon.com

WARNING:

> The following pages contain **explicit** material that is beneficial for your health

THIS BOOK EXPLAINS TECHNIQUES FOR GREATER <u>SELF-ESTEEM</u> AND <u>MENTAL TOUGHNESS</u> TO FACILITATE <u>CHANGE</u>.

WARNING:

> Using the methods contained in **the following chapters will improve** the **quality** of your life.

TABLE OF CONTENTS

Women: A Dedication 9
Preface 11
Chapter One: Women and Power 15
    Exercise: POWER OF PURPOSE 19
    Exercise: GOAL SETTING TIME LINES 21
    Exercise: USING BREATH FOR RELAXATION 23
    Exercise: SPEAK TO YOUR BRAIN 26
    Exercise: FLEXIBILITY 30
Chapter Two: The Sandwich Generation 36
    Even Eagles Need a Push 46
    The Wisdom of Eleanor Roosevelt 47
    Things My Mother Taught Me 48
Chapter Three: The Emotional Roller Coaster 49
    Exercise: CLICHÉS AND OTHER EXPRESSIONS 50
    Exercise: UNCOVERING WIDELY HELD BELIEFS 51
    Exercise: A FEEL GOOD LIST 54
    Exercise: AN INTEGRITY CHECKLIST 57
    Exercise: A SELF-ESTEEM PROFILE 60
    Strategies for Changing Your Mood 62
    Aging 63
    Personal Mapmaking: Roy Hughes Roberts 64
Chapter Four: Breaking the Stress Barrier 70
    Exercise: TIME OUT 71
    Everybody Has a Body 71
    Exercise: ENERGY BOOSTERS 73
    Exercise: END OF THE DAY 74
    Living with Compromise 75
    Cracks in Your Foundation 76
    Look at Your Little List 77
    Exercise: METAPHORS 78
    The Bright Side of Life 79

Vitality 80
 The Over-Committed, Over-Scheduled Woman: Susan
  Corbett 82
Chapter Five: Intimate Relationships 91
 Exercise: SUPERHUMAN 91
 Exercise: BALANCING RELATIONSHIPS 97
 What I've Learned 100
 The Difference Between Men and Women 102
 Relationships: Some Personal Stories 105
 Advanced Relationships: Carlos Warter, M.D. 108
Chapter Six: Midlife in the Workplace 117
 Exercise: ACCENTUATE THE POSITIVE 119
 The Path of Success 120
 Releasing Negative Thoughts Sets You Free 123
 What Do You Really Want from Your Life's Work? 124
 Five Barriers to Asking for What You Want 127
 A Woman in a Man's World: Dorothy Engels-Gulden 132
 Like Money in the Bank 140
Chapter Seven: Health—Risk and Opportunity 141
 Menopause Made Easy 141
 Self Care 143
 Osteoporosis—Are You at Risk? 148
 Self-Assessment Worksheet 152
 Seven Steps to an Energy Overhaul 155
 Aging and Reproduction: Randy S. Morris, M.D. 157
 Exercise for Health: Sean Kenny, C.P.T. 164
Chapter Eight: Becoming Me 172
 Once and Still Champion: Trish Falkner 172
 It Happens: Melissa Applegate 179
 Metamorphosis: Pat Drewry 186
Chapter Nine: Communication Beyond Words 193
 Art as an Inspirational Tool: Jacqueline Ripstein 193
 Photography as a Universal Communicator: Béla Kalman 198
 Harnessing the Healing Powers of Sound: Steven Halpern ... 201
Chapter Ten: Mid-Laugh Opportunity 209
 Using Humor to Design the Future: Steve Bhaerman 210
Editor's Epilogue: Martin Ducheny 248
About the Author 251

Women: A Dedication

- Women have strengths that amaze men. They carry children, they carry hardships, they carry burdens...but they hold happiness, love and joy.
- They smile when they want to scream. They sing when they want to cry.
- They cry when they are happy and laugh when they are nervous.
- Women wait by the phone for a "safe at home" call from a friend or child after a snowy drive home.
- They vote for the person that will do the best job for family issues.
- They walk and talk the extra mile to get their children the right schools and their families the right health care.
- They won't take "no" for an answer when they believe there is a better solution.
- They can wipe a tear, bandage a cut and pat you on the back at the same time.
- They are smart, knowing that knowledge *is* power. But they still know how to use their softer side to make a point.
- They cry when their children excel and cheer when their friends get awards.
- They get teary eyed when others do great things.
- They lend a shoulder to cry on, an ear to listen and a voice to make suggestions.
- They are strongest when there seems to be no strength left.
- They will rush to be by your side when you are lonely.
- A woman's touch can cure any ailment. They know that a hug and kiss can heal a broken heart.
- They can bring out the best in husbands, children and friends.

- They are not there to push, but to gently encourage. They are cheerleaders, teachers, lovers. They can whisper a kind word, scream a loud cheer and laugh away a fear. They can mend your broken spirit and give you back your self-esteem.
- They can be sad and hopeful at the same time.
- Women do more than just give birth. They bring joy and hope. They teach others to dream and set goals. They pass on compassion and ideals. They climb into a person's life and make everything better again. They give moral support to their family and friends. And all they want back is a hug, a smile and for you to do the same to people you come in contact with.
- Women are leaders. They want to touch you in a way that will make you share your goodness with others. One extra minute of a woman's time will make a child feel special. One more kiss will make her husband feel loved.

Preface

Life is multi-phased. The book of life has an introduction, a preface, a body, a summary and a conclusion. Inevitably every life has these chapters. The introduction is the formative influence of our family environment and our early years preparing us for the rest of our lives. The preface is the personal experimentation of early life that leads us to our identity. The body of our book is the using of the influence of our introduction and preface to grow independently by gathering and processing new information and experiences. The summary is what we pass on to our peers and to future generations. The conclusion is the personal meaning of our book of life. In a very real way, the book of life is a story of values.

As we write the body of our book, society bombards us with conflicting values. Marketing idolizes words such as *beauty, wealth, health* and *youth*. This forceful message conjures an image of rich, young women ruling the world—a message that says it is the early part of the story that contains all the value. In my experience, the real power years come later, within the midlife cycle. Midlife is a time when intellect, compassion and experience can combine with positive action to blend true authentic power.

I am in the midst of that energizing cycle. I am divorced, have two grown children and ailing parents. I have to cope with a demanding schedule, lifestyle changes, financial concerns, and the *empty nest* syndrome. Physical appearance is important to me, and it seems to take ever more effort to stay trim than it did in years past. With less time in my life, I have more sensitivity in selecting of friends and establishing relationships.

For me, this is a time for appreciation and celebration when everyday can become unique. It is a time for recognition of my children's lives and the choices that they make. I also see my parent's choices more clearly, and I am aware that sometimes in my caretaker's position I become my parents' parent. I am entwined in three generations of life, and it is indeed a special time of my life—a truly magnificent midlife experience.

Yes, some days are struggles, but each day seem to build on the next to create a pattern of growth. Lou Holtz, when he was head football coach at the University of Notre Dame, said something that summed up how I feel: "We aren't where we want to be, we aren't where we ought to be, but thank goodness we aren't where we used to be."

I hope that everyone can experience what I know to be the power of midlife women. This is why I asked a number of experts to help me create "Phenomenal Women." If you are a midlife woman, this book can be your fountain of youth, your prime-time coach, and your most supportive cheerleader. It is a source to help you get you closer to who you want to be. The chapters that follow will bring you techniques to make you aware if you are dwelling on past mistakes. They will show you optional paths to help you learn from your experiences and move on without regret. They will help you live in the present, rather than leaning on the past or existing for the future. They will teach you that nothing is all good or all bad. Life is an experience, and what we term success and failure are merely outcomes.

The techniques introduced in this book will help you think differently and continue refining your thinking to produce the results you want. It will take work, of course, but the results are waiting for you. Even if you have not had a history of personal success, tomorrow is waiting for you. As Monty Hall, the TV game show host explained, "Actually I'm an overnight success. But it took me 20 years."

You can use these chapters as your manual for fine-tuning your self-esteem and positive thinking. You will find options, procedures and exercises to build mental toughness and clarity for success. You will reawaken skills long forgotten, and you will be able to give yourself permission to be healthy, wealthy and happy. All the ingredients are here to help you learn to be pro-active and make life happen for you rather than to you.

You will start with baby steps and minimal risk taking so you can begin in your comfort zone. See how to be more flexible and go around obstacles rather than collide with them. Learn how to set up options in challenging situations to create a safety net for success. With your new *success* mentality, confidence and self-esteem are ensured.

This entire book can be your "Garden of Eden." It offers you many options for growing your seeds of awareness, imagination and experience. Within this garden you will have the desire, the ability and the technique to grow vital and strong—to be a midlife woman of power.

> *Now isn't then, and you can make anything happen with enough options.*

CHAPTER ONE

WOMEN AND POWER

The world has recognized us as a powerful generation. Midlife women can be found in politics, in the legal system, working as media producers, directors, stars, company presidents, financial advisors, lawyers, accountants, designers—the list goes on forever. Capable, intelligent, beautiful women play leadership roles throughout the world.

We look great outside because we are taking care of ourselves from the inside. We exude authentic power with compassion. What a combination! Together, they spark vibrant energy!

Many women in this cycle of life are asking the same questions:

- Question 1   Who Am I?
- Question 2   What do I stand for?
- Question 3   What is my purpose?
- Question 4   Where am I going?
- And the basic underlying question—I've lived almost half of my life, and am I happy?

Here are some thoughts on these questions. When I ask the **first question,** "Who am I?" I think I am referring to something solid enough—my identity; but I can't begin to answer that question without multiple frames of reference. My combined sense of identity organizes my beliefs, capabilities, and behaviors into a single system; yet that singularity can limit me more than liberate me. Have I included enough information to answer or resolve such a puzzle?

My genetic and hereditary makeup, environmental input (family, social, economic status), and the sum accumulation of experiences contribute to my feelings of identity; yet my identity keeps changing as my experiences keep changing. If someone were to meet me after a fifteen-year hiatus and said that I haven't changed a bit, I'd be upset. Maybe I would like some aspects to have changed and some not. I would love to look the same physically, but I would want to keep today's growth and maturity. Maturity is the balance between courage and consideration.

I thrive on change. I enjoy learning and then putting this new learning into action to see results in myself. Patience is a big lesson for me, because I love instant gratification.

So who am I? Can I answer that question in ways that don't limit my options?

> It's not how old you are, but how you are old.
> — Marie Dressler

Who do you think you are? Who would you like to become? Have you considered more than what appeals to your fantasies? What would you have to do to be yourself and how would you know when you got there?

The **second question** is, "What do I stand for?" We each hold many individual beliefs, standards and values. Our experiences, to date, came from billions of beliefs—about our body, intellectual worth, and about how attractive we feel. We fashion our principles from our religion, our notions of sin, our beliefs about our mortality, from the values we connect to family, to society, to government, etc. We treat these beliefs as truths, and our mind holds onto them with great determination.

When you look at what you believe, you may find that much of it came from lessons you learned—something you were taught and got an "A" for knowing—or are due to something you learned the hard way, at one time, in one situation. The past may have little or no foundation in your circumstances today. You do not rectify what you did *then* by doing it again *now*. You can not make over what you didn't do before by doggedly doing it now. You are a transitional person, a link between the past and the future. Your decisions can change the world.

Recognize your "response-ability"—the ability to choose your response—being pro-active. In choosing a response to a situation, you affect the outcome. We should use our beliefs to guide and interpret our perceptions of reality, not to deny or distort them. If we misuse our beliefs, as filters or blinders, we seek and find evidence to support our misuse and might retreat into make-believe. We could then say that we lack a valid reality check. What we are actually doing is creating our own data to support exactly what we think we want.

We each hold our values, ideals and ethics in great esteem—and often charge them with rich emotion. From them, we fashion rules, standards and principles. We define levels of quality and form bases for comparison. We then construct idealized versions of what we believe we need in order to feel satisfied, honorable or comfortable. In the past, we held on like bulldogs to these beliefs or values that we had infused with intense emotion. As midlife women, we have more focus. We can reconsider clearly, replacing intensity with calm. Happily, our years have given us reserves of calmness and pockets of serenity to draw upon. We have made rules, but we have learned how to change them for our benefit. Now we can learn to tap our accumulated reserves of energy and experience.

When we combine our beliefs, values and standards, we integrate our internal system for decision making. This system is what we use to think and process information. It provides the reasoning behind why we behave as we do and why we take the actions that we do.

In order to change any actions, we must change our process of thinking. Our identity is created by the way we organize our thinking patterns. Everything we do starts out as a thought form, and then we take action to make it happen. For instance, a building is first a thought before it can be constructed. A vacation first starts as a thought, and then we make it reality. Likewise, anything else we create

is a thought form first, and we then figure out how to bring it to physical form.
Think of your beliefs, your values and your standards. Do any aspects need attention? Which areas? Let your belief system be beneficial for you. The only way to act differently is to think differently.

> *Every solution starts out as a challenge, so life is a flip chart of challenges to be met and goals to become accomplished.*

The **third question** is, "What is my purpose?" This is where intention links with ability to generate goals. Self-talk determines our attitudes and thoughts, which in turn determine the behaviors we employ to strive for results. We are constantly setting up goals, attaining them and moving on. A challenge mastered is a solution. Then the next challenge arises.

Our major or essential purpose in life becomes more apparent as we search through the accumulation of our experiences. It becomes a knowing that just feels right at the soul level. We hear an inside "yes." As we transform closer to our true identity, the purer and more satisfying our goals become. Then our goals are satisfying at the physical, emotional, mental *and* spiritual levels.

To find your purpose, examine what activities give you a sense of meaning Earlier in life, we first wanted the approval of friends, family and society. Now we are looking for purposes that are personally meaningful. Living with purpose is a matter of living with the awareness of who we are and what we want.

I consider that my purpose is to empower myself so I can give options to others for self-empowerment. Think about what your purposes are. Why do you feel this way? What can you do to transform your purposes into goals?

Many peak performers in any field are visualizers. They see, feel and otherwise experience reaching their goals before they actually do it. They begin with the end in mind. For you to do this yourself, create an internal *comfort zone* or *sacred space* for yourself and imagine what you desire. The more elaborately you create the image, the greater will be your commitment to make it happen. When you identify what really matters to you, you will start to think in grander terms. An effective goal focuses on the end rather than on the means. It identifies where you want to be and helps you determine where you are in relation to it. This is a sure way to generate the energy that will give life to your effort.

Exercise: POWER OF PURPOSE

It may take weeks, months or years of experience to determine your purpose. Defining personal and professional purpose must come from within. Start by quietly asking questions and listening for answers. Here are some possible questions to help find your purpose:

1. What is meaningful in my life?
2. What are my beliefs about:
    Family—Others—Power
    Finances—Sexuality—Love
    Self—Relationships—Intimacy
    Work—Health—Mortality
3. What are my short-term goals?
4. What are my long-term goals?
5. What are my values?
6. What are my standards?
7. What skills do I have?
8. What skills do I want?
9. How can I make a difference?

After you have listened for the answers to come to you, complete this statement: My purpose in life is:

* * *

The **fourth question** is, "Where am I going?" This question builds on a compilation of the first three answers. First we have to determine who we are (identity), what our belief systems are (how we think and feel), and what our purposes are. Then we can decide how to react to what we have discovered. We create our future through every decision that we make from that point on, therefore, every decision becomes a precious target for opportunity.

Where do you want to go with your life? What do you have to think and do to make that journey a reality? Every big idea starts as a small one.

> We have the vitality of youth and the maturity of experience to create whatever we want and need.

Take baby steps to start, but start. Success is not a destination, it's a joy ride. If you do not find the journey to be largely fun, you are probably headed to the wrong place.

> Don't think of one hundred reasons why you can't do what you want to; find one reason why you can.

Exercise: GOAL SETTING TIME LINES

Focus on three different time frames for setting goals.

    Short term—30 days or less

1.
2.
3.
4.
5.

    Medium term—1 month to 12 months

6.
7.
8.
9.
10.

    Long term—more than one year

11.
12.
13.
14.

* * *

The **final question**—and probably the one that drives us to ask all the other questions—is, "Having lived almost half my life, am I happy?" Happiness, of course, is an inside job. Optimists pass over possibilities of failure while pessimists exaggerate them. We usually measure our success externally—an outside-in comparison—but no one feels successful this way all the time. We must continually reevaluate our measure for happiness. On the other hand, if we have peace of mind, we are continually content and happy. *This happiness comes from within.* Peace of mind does not come about by removing all stress—something that is impossible anyway. It comes from being content in spite of the stress. In that peaceful frame of mind we are able to make positive decisions. Happiness is a mind-set.

Whenever you don't feel wonderful, acknowledge that the unhappy feeling is merely a mood. Observe it. Examine it. Then learn how to get back to that feeling of peace. What seemed a major calamity when you are distressed and in doubt may just be a minor setback when you are at peace. Life is a pendulum of moods. By noticing when the pendulum swings off center and pulling it back quickly, you can make life blissful. Make the most of any unhappy mood by learning from it. Then get back to your center for HAPPINESS, CONTENTMENT AND JOY.

Use these questions as your compass to chart your journey toward the new you:

- Who am I?
- What is my purpose?
- What do I stand for?
- Where am I going?
- Now that I have lived almost half my life, am I happy?

> *Goals are what we aim for. Plans are what we do.*

There are times when WE MAJOR IN MINOR THINGS. We worry too much about things that may never happen or blow them way out of proportion. Those are the times to realize that worry is a darkroom where negatives are developed. It really is no big deal. One way to get to do something right is to do it wrong—only don't let it take too long—and try again. Here is something else to help you return to your center if you have been knocked off course.

Exercise: USING BREATH FOR RELAXATION

This type of breathing soothes and releases tensions. The relaxation it generates calms body interference and mental chatter and allows you to function in the present rather than being stuck in the past or the future.
Place your hands under your rib cage with your fingertips touching. Inhale while sending the air down to your fingertips. As you feel your diaphragm expanding, your ribs and chest separate and your fingers come slightly apart. Inhale slowly to the count of four. As you do this, think of the breath as a vitalizing factor and reconfirm it by visualizing pure air going throughout you with every breath. Hold the breath to the count of four. Exhale to the count of eight. Your fingertips come back together again as your chest lowers. Visualize that all negativity, toxins and problems are released with this exhalation. Breathing in and holding the breath should be the same count, while the exhalation is double that amount. So the proportion is 4-4-8. When that becomes easy, increase the count to 5-5-10, then to 6-6-12, etc. The slower you breathe, the more beneficial it will be. This should not be used only as an exercise, but it should become your normal way of breathing.

* * *

The four questions presented in this chapter—along with the grand question of "Am I happy?"—are really the basis for this entire book. Take the time to answer them. Record your answers in a place where you can refer back to them for revisions. As you learn to think differently, you will have more opportunities to create the quality, excitement and adventure in the life you are now shaping. *Change your thoughts and you will change your future!*
This analogy helps explain it all. Think for a moment of a tomato plant. In order to get hundreds of tomatoes; one must start with a small, dried seed. That seed doesn't look like a tomato plant, but when you plant it in fertile soil, water it and let the sun shine on it, that tiny seed becomes

a short shoot that grows into a plant. Pull away the weeds that might choke it, continue watering the plant as it becomes stronger—and see all the tomatoes that come from that one seed.

It is the same with creating a new life experience. The soil in which you plant your dreams is your subconscious mind. The seed is a new thought or new way of being you. The whole new life experience ahead exists in the potential of this tiny seed—if you keep it watered with positive thoughts, and if you continually weed your garden by pulling out the negative thoughts. Then watch your dream seed manifest itself because of all your care and nurturing.

Once we have discovered this capability, we owe it to ourselves to be as successful in every area as we can. Why now? *As midlife women, we are in our most powerful cycle of life.* We have the ability, the intelligence and the capability to create whatever lifestyle we want. In order to know what we *do* want, clear out what is not needed for a true weeding out process. What remains after the weeding will be the sturdy stem and branches of our visions that will blossom and bear fruit.

As your coach, I offer you this great advice. *Become aware* of the conditioned patterns of thought and behavior that no longer benefit you; then *take action* to change them to what you want and need.

Here are some potential thought-traps that need attention so you can avoid them throughout life. As you spot and avoid the traps, you will develop greater insight, and with it a greater ability to draw on your accumulated experiences for change.

1. *We expect the future to be like the past.* Although we remember what we liked in the past and try to project that into the future, we must realize that we can't walk backwards into the future. Use the successful aspects from your past, but choose only those that are still viable in present situations to help create your new future.
2. *We work hard to manipulate and control our immediate world.* This only keeps us in our comfort zone and may not be beneficial for our growth. Take some risks, be

flexible and flow with the situation. Life is an adventure, and the nature of adventure is that it is always, to some extent, out of control.
3. *We present ourselves in ways that are different from how we are really feeling.* This creates a dichotomy and a dilemma inside of us. Notice when these *masks* are worn and why. Know that it is fine to be who you are and be proud of what you feel.
4. *When we don't feel loved, we try to control the external circumstances we believe are causing the unhappiness.* Love and happiness are inside jobs. We must create them for ourselves.
5. *We believe that living is a matter of surviving, not of growing.* The tragedy of life is not that it ends so soon, but that we may wait so long to begin it. Midlife is prime time. Draw upon all life's experiences to gain knowledge and to experience the vitality of living fully.
6. *We can take comfort in the consistency of our unhappiness and pain.* Many feel that they are only alive in the midst of a crisis so they precipitate one crisis after another to experience life. You are the writer, the director, the producer and the principal actor in your individual play called life. It is your choice to script each day as a comedy, a tragedy, an adventure or a love story.
7. *Our prejudices protect us.* There would actually be very little to dislike in others if we didn't bring to them our own judgments and petty grievances. We judge what we like and don't like through our own filters of right and wrong. If you realize that every person is scripting his or her life according to an individually set scenario and timetable, you may see them differently.
8. *Knowledge is power.* While that is true, unless you see the importance of consistency in what you think, say and *do*—your progress will be slow in changing your attitudes for more positive approaches. Lots of people KNOW what to do, but few people DO what they know.
9. *The world is cruel and unforgiving.* It is easy to blame the world, but the world is what you make of it. If you are not convinced of the real potential of your future suc-

cess, it will elude you. We can only grow effectively with a mindset that is geared for success. In other words, our thinking determines how effective our decisions will be.

Exercise: SPEAK TO YOUR BRAIN

The brain weighs less than three pounds and, in the adult, comprises less than 8.5 percent of our weight.

We conceive of our brain as a thinking instrument that is essentially rational and logical. Tests generally measure our intellect but they don't test the creative aspects of the person. By just merely showing the brain attention, more blood goes to the brain, and with it goes oxygen. The oxygen stimulates the brain cells into rejuvenation and can produce clearer, more effective thinking.

Your unconscious is like a computer that is programmed by your thoughts. Therefore, wrong doing is only the result of wrong thinking. If you don't like the results, you must change your thinking to produce the outcomes that you do want. It is said that we have a negative thought about ourselves every few minutes. Monitor your thoughts. Write down any that are negative about yourself. Do this for one full week and notice if you are building a self-destruct mentality. You must reinforce the positive thoughts or you will be strengthening the negative ones instead.

* * *

We must each be pro-active in order to have life *respond* to us instead of having life's events *happen* to us. This story illustrates the point. Scott's mother called him to wake up and go to school. There was no answer so she called again. No answer. Going upstairs she now screamed his wake up call and shook him out of sleep. He awoke and said that he wasn't going to go to school anymore. He said that there were a thousand kids at that school and they all hated him.

His mother stood her ground and insisted that he go anyway. Scott protested again, now stating that all the teachers hate him as well. He noticed a group of them talking about him, and he just wasn't going. His mother now yelled, "Get to school!" Frustrated, Scott just couldn't understand why she would want him to go into such a hostile environment. His mother replied, "For two good reasons. First, you are 40 years old. Second, you are the principal."

At times we have all felt like Scott. We just don't want to go to school. School is actually life, and sometimes we would rather exist than *live life* and face the challenges that come with it.

> Don't do things not to die, but to live.

Every challenge is an opportunity to grow; yet often we act as if by ignoring the challenges, the uncomfortable pressure to grow into someone new will just disappear. There is no such thing as a vacuum in this universe. Nothing disappears without something else taking its place. The thing that takes the place of growth is death. By willingly embracing all the challenges that come our way, we give ourselves the chance to be fully alive rather than passing time and waiting to die.

We usually face these challenges through two basic emotions—LOVE or FEAR. These are the foundation of all the other emotions. We move toward anybody or any circumstance that we enjoy out of love and move away from what we dislike out of fear. Both of these emotions are responsive inventions of the mind. What we fear in one stage of life may bring us great joy in another. What is an attraction for one person can elicit fear from another. For instance, I love to speak in front of an audience. For many people this would be a very fearful prospect, and they would go to great lengths to avoid it.

It is merely our internal consideration of a situation that labels it as good or bad, harmful or wonderful. In actuality, the label flows entirely from our *perception* of what the facts are, and not the facts themselves.

Consideration of actual facts is called *Objective Thinking*. Our opinion of the facts is our *Subjective Thinking*. Being able to separate objective from subjective thinking, while often difficult in practice, can make life much simpler.

Here is a simple example. *Fact*—It is raining. (objective). We can view the day as awful or wonderful (subjective). Ducks would probably love it. Farmers might also love it. The personal spin that we put on the facts determines whether we see the rain as good, bad or irrelevant. Therefore, it is what we do with the facts that count. Another example: The woman is beautiful. The fact is that she is a woman (objective). Our opinion is that she is beautiful (subjective).

What we experience seems to be real because it reflects what we want to believe. This is because our interpretive filters stand between us and a clear picture of any objective reality. When people are asked to comment on a certain situation, some very different honestly held viewpoints come forward. To illustrate:

There were three people in a store, a detective, a fashion designer and a dentist. A man came in, stole some money and ran out. When the police interviewed the witnesses, the detective was very precise with details about both the crime and the perpetrator, the fashion designer remembered what the thief was wearing and the dentist remembered almost nothing.

Since everyone's individual reality is subjective, the world we see is typically a projection of our inner thoughts and wishes. To create the future we desire, we must envision our world as clearly as possible so we can start living in it.

When we are unkind to ourselves, we automatically perceive an unkind world, and we will create the evidence to back up this conviction. For instance: If you wake up and feel it's going to be a horrendous day, you will notice all the day's negative aspects and create a self-fulfilling prophecy. If you feel it will be a great day, you scan for the positive aspects, and the day turns out to be great. Whatever we direct our attention toward is emphasized. Notice where you are focusing your attention. Is this energy well spent?

> Anaïs Nin summarized this perfectly: "We don't see things as they are, we see things as we are."

For the first half of our lives we are entwined in this type of survival thinking. Most of it is at a subconscious level. Each of us has an inner essence, and, during our formative years, our ego creates an image of how we want others to perceive us.

When entering into midlife with maturity, these self-created ego boundaries disappear, and the real person "ME" starts to emerge. *Midlife is then considered an oasis instead of crises.* We are often beyond the basic survival issues that make the early years so anxious. Instead of just concentrating on each individual aspect of life, we have the foresight to look at the whole picture to see what needs adjusting.

> We are now at our peak!

Going back to the analogy of the tomato plant, when the tomato plant grows, all the individual parts have a sequential time period to mature. It may be the development of the roots, the start of the leaves, a strong stem to hold it all, and the blossoms, which later become tomatoes. Nature takes care of itself. As we mature, we also have various parts that need nurturing, stabilizing and attention. However, it is at midlife that this all comes together and aspects of our mental, emotional, and physical parts have developed and are aligned for success. It is all preparation up to this point. Now it is time to reap the benefits from our experiences.

Just as the seed of the tomato plant contains the entire plant system, *we are born as pure potential with limitless knowledge and capabilities.* There has never been and never will be the combination of molecules and atoms that is another you. Our job is to live out that unique potential. At birth our mind is a computer without programming. Our disk is blank and each of us formats and programs our own data throughout life. The hard drive remains the same, but the software is constantly changing. As we fine-tune our programming, we come closer to the identity that is *me*.

Exercise: FLEXIBILITY

In order to get what you do want; you must disable and deny what you don't want. Place this stop order on unwanted conditions by declaring that they are finished. Since it is necessary to let go of the past in order to do something different in the future, you must release any emotional attachment to situations or people that are no longer beneficial in your life. When you take something away, something else is always going to fill the space. Be sure that what is taking the empty place is strengthening you.

Many times we think we are feeling our feelings while we are merely *thinking about them*. Be aware of how you want to feel and switch gears if what you feel is not to your liking. Get a picture of what you want, set your goal, then put your cause into motion by directing your mind to think positively about the goal. As you think of what you do want, clean out your thoughts and give up old images if they no longer suit you. Be flexible so that you are open to change easily to what is best for you now. If you do not develop this flexibility, you may be cemented into the past with goals that are no longer effective for the present. This way you can create each day the way you want it to be and leave the past behind.

* * *

We are born flexible in our joints and muscles as well as in our opinions and thoughts. With age we tend to become less flexible in both our body and mind. The more rigid we become, less of the life force flows through us. Total rigidity of muscles and joints are death to those parts. It is overwhelmingly important to remain fluid, active and full of life in both mind and body.

> *We want rigor, not rigor mortis.*

At birth, females have the characteristics of woman—some of these traits are for nurturing, caring, giving, and healing. We nurture friends and family, reach out to the community and then the world. We have compassion for all creatures, and a direct connection to mother earth with the intention to make things better.

> *Women are the natural umbilical cords of the world.*

In the process of nurturing, we sometimes forget to take care of ourselves. The number one concern and responsibility is *me, myself and I* because I cannot give to others what I do not have. If I get love only 50 percent of the time and keep giving anyway, I will soon become depleted. Only when I get 100 percent of what I personally need can I give my optimum to others. Output cannot exceed input. This means that if it is not coming in, it is not going to be going out. The dictionary defines *selfish* as being devoted to and caring only for oneself. When we do that, selfishness becomes a negative trait. Being selfish is positive, however, if it means getting what we need so that we can give more to others without becoming depleted. Our energy is the replenishing of abundance that keeps flowing in and out of our lives.

Looking back at my first forty years, I was caught up in *ME*. I thought the media was right and that the young women of the world reigned. Being thin and beautiful was in vogue. The advertisers and the media portrayed these gorgeous, silken-haired, perfectly coifed women up, wearing sexy clothes, drinking fine wine, dining in great restaurants with wonderful food and being escorted by great looking gentleman. The advertisements said that this could be us if we talked a certain way, smelled great, deodorized constantly, sprayed our hair until we put holes in the ozone layer, ate certain foods, etc.

I was much more interested in the physical, the sexual, the fun, dating and whatever made *me, me, me* happy rather than developing the spiritual and conscious part of myself. I have always been a caretaker and a giver; yet my happiness depended on external influences. As I matured (I use that term because growing biologically older does not necessarily mean maturing), I realized that I was the only one responsible for my own happiness. The way to accomplish that was from the inside out and not the other way around. Somewhere along my timeline an *aha!* flashed through my mind, and I knew that I had millions of experiences upon which to choose. I was an encyclopedia of knowledge and that I had the capabilities to do whatever was necessary to program my mind and emotions. Even though my formative years were much more shallow and outside-oriented, now I was learning how to be calm at will and how to switch emotions to benefit me

I now can clearly see that everything is *attitude!* Developing the right attitude allows all your mental, physical and emotional aspects to be aligned for authentic self-power. Attitude is what makes a woman sexy and attractive. The right attitude can get you anything you desire. When you are aware that you can consciously create effective thinking, you are then truly powerful, a *femme fatale*.

Our particular midlife generation is unique. We are basically the first generation to have had more than a high school education, and to have the opportunity for a career or training before or while being married. Many of us had children in our early twenties and continued working or stayed at home to be housewives. We were so young and innocent that it was like children taking care of children, yet we felt so grown up. It would have been more comforting if our babies came with a "how to" manual, but then there was Dr. Spock, and we referred to this book like the bible.

Soon we found that someone else's knowledge could take us just so far, and that everything we learn in life, we learn by trial and error. That is, we only learn through our mistakes.

The Chinese symbol for *crisis* is made up from the characters for *danger* and *opportunity*. If you stay in your comfort zone, you receive positive feedback, and that may make you feel good, but by avoiding danger you also avoid opportunity. When you try something new, you will probably not succeed the first few times and that can hurt your ego. You must realize, however, that a real winner continues until she is successful.

Our brains contain billions of neurons, each having the ability to connect with other neurons. This is a phenomenal network of intelligence that enables us to have great potential. Winners know this and that is why they are successful. Mistakes really don't matter. What matters are to learn from the mistakes, move on and grow. Experience can be the best teacher if we reflect on it. After all we can only be prepared for the portion of our life we have already lived.

> *Success is not a destination that you ever reach.*
> *Success is the quality of your journey.*
>
> *— Jennifer James*

This story exemplifies what I mean. A successful executive was being questioned by his employee and was asked to what he attributed his success? The executive said, "That's easy to answer. It was from making good decisions." Then the employee asked, "And to what do you attribute your good decisions?" "That's easy also," the executive said, "The wisdom gained from experience." Not satisfied, the employee then asked, "And where did you get that experience?" The executive scratched his chin and thought for a moment. "I guess it was learning from bad decisions."

Here is another story that might help you understand how vitally important each day, each moment is in your process of growing the real you. An elderly carpenter was ready to retire. He told his contractor-employer of his plans to leave the house-building business and live a more leisurely life with his wife, enjoying his extended family. He would miss the paycheck, but he needed to retire. The business would have to get by without him. The contractor was sorry to see his good worker go and asked if he could build just one more house as a personal favor. The carpenter said yes, but in time it was easy to see that his heart was not in his work. His workmanship became shoddy and accepted inferior materials he would formerly have rejected. It was an unfortunate way to end his career. When the carpenter finished his work and his employer came to inspect the house, the contractor handed the front-door key to the carpenter. "This is your house," he said, "my gift to you."

What a shock! What a shame! If he had only known he was building his own house, he would have done it all so differently. Now he had to live in the home he had built none too well.

So it is with us. If we build our lives in a distracted way, reacting rather than acting, willing to put up less than the best, we will be disappointed. If, at critical points we do not give the job our best effort, then with a shock we will find that we are now living in the shoddy house we have built. If we had realized, we would have done it differently.

Think of yourself as the carpenter. Think about your house. Each day you hammer a nail, place a board or erect a wall. Build wisely. It is the masterpiece of your life that you are building. Even if you live it for only one day more, that day deserves to be lived in the dream house of your making.

Like the carpenter's house, life is a do-it-yourself project, and you must build it. Your life today is the result of your attitudes and choices in the past. Your life tomorrow will be the result of your attitudes and choices of today.

Unlike the carpenter, you have the opportunity to rebuild your dream house with full knowledge that it is for you to live in.

We are in the prime of our lives, and every choice we make is an opportunity for the happiness and success that we deserve. More than at any time of our lives, we have the knowledge, the resources, the capabilities, the vitality and the power to create abundance in every aspect of life. *Use life up!* The richest places on earth are the cemeteries because so many dreams and ideas are buried there. Go for your dreams and live life.

> In the words of Mae West,
> "Too much of a good thing can be wonderful!"

Please keep referring to this chapter and learn the methods presented here. They are a great resource for building your foundation for self-esteem and awareness. The chapters that follow will help you learn how to add the frame, walls, roof and all the rest of your personal dream.

Chapter Two

The Sandwich Generation

We are the largest, most powerful, knowledgeable group of women in American history.

Statistics show that between World War II and 1964, 78 million people were born in the United States. Four out of ten people are now between the ages of 35 and 54, and this population will increase 20 percent between 1995 and the year 2000. Every 7.5 seconds another person turns 50, and more than fifty percent of those are women. As empty nesters, our generation has more money to spend and our median income is greater than that of any other generation.

The increased educational level alone is revolutionizing the midlife market. Add to that the factors of working women, widespread divorce, individualistic attitudes, small families and dual incomes, and we have an entirely new recipe for consumer marketing. Three decades ago marketers created the youth market. Now in *Mid-youth*, as American Demographics Magazine referred to us in 1995, we still have many of the same wants and needs we had in our youth. We want fun, and our lifelong search for a good time is directly related to our strong sense of individualism.

According to Cheryl Russell in *American Demographics*, we are unlike any previous generation. She states that we will be turning consumer markets upside down. For years we have suppressed our individualistic natures raising children—often single-handedly. With our children grown, we can spend on ourselves again.

Cheryl continues saying that our generation has upped the divorce rate. Many more women head their own households and have become the matriarchs of families consisting of grown children and stepchildren, grandchildren, in-laws and ex-in-laws, nieces, nephews and close friends. Almost one in five households headed by a 45- to 60-year-old woman includes adult children. This proportion has been rising because today's young adults are slower to leave home than we were. Many of us welcome the emotional and economic support of this ever-changing, multi-generation household.

While writing this book I began to realize the differences in philosophies, morals and ethics between our generation, the one preceding ours (our parents') and the one after (our children's). I am fascinated by how we can so clearly identify our era as distinctly different. We have been on the leading edge of educational opportunities, civil rights advances and technological improvements. Some of us marched on Washington in protest of war; at another time we frolicked in the mud at Woodstock.

One of the strongest influences from our youth was the conflict in Vietnam. Protesting the war may have been viewed as unpatriotic, but it was our brothers, boyfriends or husbands going off to war and sometimes not returning. Many of the men who returned were not the same people we knew. They had drastically changed, and we changed with them.

We launched men into space, and science fiction became reality. The space trips became longer culminating in visits to the moon. Timothy Leary led the way in experimentation with mind-altering drugs; from this the drug culture was born. The birth control pill became available, and women became sexually freer. We soon saw hippies and free love—and we thought we had all the answers.

Now, some of us are teachers, doctors, lawyers and grandparents, and, as the future emerges, we are the generation who may bankrupt Social Security.

To sensitize you to the many cultural elements that have formed how you think and feel today, consider these icons and see how many ring a familiar note.

People: Marilyn Monroe, Twiggy, James Dean, Marlon Brando, John Wayne, Roy Rogers and Dale Evans, Jerry Lewis, Dean Martin, Sammy Davis Jr., Frank Sinatra, The Rat Pack, Elizabeth Taylor, Richard Burton, Rock Hudson, Doris Day, Little Richard, Duke Ellington, Jane Fonda, Gloria Steinam, Hugh Heffner, Albert Einstein, Jonas Salk, and Martin Luther King.

Moments: Sputnik, the Apollo Program, bra burning, J.F. Kennedy murdered, Berlin Wall, Cuban missile crisis, Vietnam, Cassius Clay becomes Mohammed Ali, Billie Jean King beats Bobbie Riggs in the tennis battle of the sexes, Cold War, Iron Curtain, and transcendental meditation.

TV programs: Flash Gordon, Mousekateers, American Bandstand, Howdy Doody. Dragnet, Mod Squad, Candid Camera, I Love Lucy, The Little Rascals, Ed Sullivan, Milton Berle, The Honeymooners, Gunsmoke, Brady Bunch, Taxi, Mash, and Father Knows Best.

Icons for our generation: bell bottoms, mini skirts, Motown, Rhythm and Blues, tie died clothing, flower children, flower power, bikinis, platform shoes, V.W. Bug, psychedelic art, disco, doo wop music, hula hoops, Nehru jackets, beatniks, penny loafers, Woodstock, hot pants, Liverpool, Schmoo, Slinky, Etch-a-sketch, peace signs, Afro hairdos, saddle shoes, bobby socks, poodle skirts, black and white TV, transistor radios, rotary telephones, flattops, D.A. haircut, abortion issues, "I like Ike," the women's movement, women's rights, crinolines, Dr. Spock, terms such as *groovy, neat, funky*, unit air-conditioning in homes, roll up windows in cars, manual convertible tops, hippies, and free love.

Shows and Movies: *Hair, Oh Calcutta, Jesus Christ Superstar, On the Waterfront, Giant, Dr. Zhivago, Sound of Music, The King and I, Rear View Mirror, Psycho, Cleopatra, Shane,* and *The Ten Commandments*.

Musical Groups: KC and the Sunshine Band, The Fifth Dimension, The Platters, The Righteous Brothers, The Four Tops, The Beatles, Elvis Presley, Johnny Cash, Hank Williams, Liberace, Mario Lanza, and Margo Fontaine.

Songs: *Earth Angel, Unchained Melody, My Prayer, Peppermint Twist, Purple People Eater, Itsie Bitsy Teeny Weenie Yellow Polka Dot Bikini, Jail House Rock.*

Dances: Mashed Potato, The Fish, The Hully Gully, The Twist, The Swim, and The Stroll.

The memories go on. Add to the list, and have fun reminiscing.

As I was making out my list, I was reliving an era that was one of innocence and purity. The humor, the movies, and the music depicted ethics, morals, standards, and stereotypes that were very definitely right or wrong.

We had taken on the philosophy of our parents without realizing that we had ingested—and were actually following—their unwritten rules and regulations.

> *In buying someone else's philosophy, we are also buying the consequences.*

In early youth, we were "good" girls. We would never think of living with a man before marriage. We didn't sleep around, and actual sexual intercourse rarely occurred before marriage. We had milestones called first, second and third base—and I'm not talking about baseball. We played sports, had a childhood and were teenagers. We looked and acted our age and weren't particularly sophisticated. We were taught manners. We learned to be nice little girls growing up in an era that had very definite ethical codes.

Most of our mothers never went beyond high school. We would become the first generation of women to have widespread college education. Many of us got married right after school and had a child by the time we were in our mid-twenties. We were family-minded, not career-oriented. Our dream life was to get married, have children, live in a house in the country and be a homemaker.

There were few opportunities for women in careers. We could be secretaries, nurses, teachers, salespeople, but we still couldn't climb up the corporate ladder. Wages were lower for women doing the same jobs as men.

In the 1980s and 1990s, job opportunities expanded and women could become anything they wanted. We now studied law and medicine and became integrated into corporate management or built our own companies.

Through higher education and the effects of the women's movement, we were striving for more independence and equality. We were moving out of household chores and participating in community, state and global issues. We became a voice to be reckoned with. By integrating and participating in the community and world affairs, women became more independent—emotionally, mentally and financially. Although the husband's role was still that of a provider, we now were providing very well on our own. We were looking for relationships to be the way we wanted them to be, we were working in higher paying jobs, and we were becoming much more flexible in our ideas of what we could and would do with our lives. Rather than black and white, our world was becoming shades of gray.

Women were choosing their sexual preferences and living life as a single woman, single parent, bisexual, lesbian, heterosexual or any other way they wished. We became more health conscious, in tune with nature; youth oriented, and well-traveled, and we began looking forward to an early retirement to enjoy life. We learned that if we expect to do well, we will; and we started expecting and doing.

Midlife is this great opportunity for personal growth, enrichment and autonomy. The first forty years were preparation. We now have the ability to draw from our experiences to cope with life's challenges. This knowledge gives us strength and builds success mentality. Youth has everything to do with enthusiasm and energy and much less to do with chronological age. We don't have to act our biological age; it's how young we think and feel that counts.

> *Each day toss out one aspect of your life that causes you difficulty and you will see progress!*

We will never be part of the "mature" market as in previous generations because our attitudes about life are continually new and vibrant. We are individualistic, independent and self-indulgent. Many of the challenges of midlife center around families, relationships, jobs and personal health. As a result, sales of skin creams, suntan lotions, hair coloring, cosmetics, vitamins, and nutritional supplements are surging as a preventative against the aging process. Self-help and spirituality are priorities as we search for life's meaning.

We are also coming to see the full scope of life. The death of a parent is usually one of the traumatic events we encounter. This awakening to our own mortality tends to shift our priorities to inward balance and peace. Many midlife women also experience their first serious illness. As the threat of chronic illness rises, priorities shift again.

I have referred to us as the "sandwich generation," as we are the transitional generation. As I stated in the introductory chapter, *"This is a time for celebration. It is a time for recognition of my children's choices and my parent's choices. Sometimes there is a role reversal with my taking the caretaker's position. I am therefore entwined in three phases of life skills all creating a pattern for future growth. It is indeed a special time of my life. A truly magnificent midlife experience."*

Another metaphor for our generation is to visualize us as the *waist* of an hourglass. The top globe of the hourglass represents the previous generation and the lower globe represents the succeeding generation with our era between them. We have the advantage of reaping their wisdom and values and then passing it on to our children and our children's children.

Many of our parents were not born in the United States. They came here enmeshed in traditions that were both ethically and morally unquestionable. There was right and wrong with little room for flexibility. Role models were very specific, and everyone knew what was expected. There was a *correct* way to think and behave. Most women did not have a higher education. Their lives centered on children and family rather than career. This was the attitude and environment that encompassed our growing up.

Jane Aberlin at eighty-five is the author of *Seniority Rules* which is a light look at longevity. Jane has been a participant at my seminars for the last four years and certainly has a lust for life.

Quoting from Jane's book: " Why did I bother to write this book? What is the point? Then I realized that everyone wants to learn about his or her roots. I am often asked as my grandchildren grow into adolescence, 'What was it like before TV, computers, supermarkets, recycling and all the rest?' These little essays and comments are my gift of the past to the future. They are my continuing legacy for my grandchildren and their children as they plough through the wilderness of the twenty-first century."

Jane is talking about her essays being a gift. I view our generation as the gift between the two eras. We are passing the treasures and knowledge from the previous generation forward to the next generation as keepsakes and to continue preserving them for the future.

Jane continues: "Most young people today cherish mementos—the silver candlesticks packed lovingly and brought to America from some foreign country, the linens in a long forgotten hope chest, the Victorian silver, lamps, and photo albums. My daughter was able to use her great-grandmother's wedding ring. Because it was a wide old-fashioned band, we had room to engrave her wedding date above the original one, November 24, 1888."

"Looking at my scrapbook, I know that this may be better than silver or dishes or antique jewelry…this is, in fact, my immortality. Perhaps this is the best we can do for any of our progeny. Perhaps it is enough. None of us has a crystal ball. But words neither bend, nor break, nor disappear. Each of us can give this personal legacy of memory and love to those who come after."

We are that living legacy that Jane is referring to. We are that bridge between the generations. Especially now, in midlife, we have so much more to draw from and give out to our children. We give mementos from our past as treasures in the present to keep memories alive in the future. The wedding ring that Jane mentioned is now being worn two generations later. This is just one example of a wonderful energy connection. Gifts that are passed through the generations are priceless. The truth of the words "the more things change, the more they stay the same" becomes clearer to us as we take tremendous effort to connect to our roots.

We grew up as *proper* little girls. Then newfound freedom of choice and thought allowed us much more flexibility in every aspect of our lives than the previous generation knew. Comparing the movies, plays, songs and lifestyle of our era to that of our parents clearly shows the major changes in just one generation.

> It was not until I reached middle age that I had the courage to develop interests of my own, outside of my duties to my family.
> — Eleanor Roosevelt

Since the introduction of new medications, better nutrition, more effective exercising and a healthier way of living, we are living longer. Our parents may be belly dancing, hot air ballooning, bungee jumping, playing golf and tennis and living with more enthusiasm than previous generations. Yet, there comes a time when vitality begins to wane, and they need help. We, their children, now take the parental role. We are making decisions for their care, physical health, financial obligations and general well-being.

> A body is a place that memories call home.

The parents who nurtured us are now being nurtured by us. The values, standards and beliefs that were instilled in us by them arise again. It is time to honor them for all they gave us throughout our formative years.

It seems unnatural to be parenting our own parents. Somehow we always expect to feel like a child and have them guide us no matter how old we are. Because we have now experienced so many of life's challenges, we can empathize with and relate to our parents with compassion and understanding. We can realize how much they had given to us, sacrificing their own needs to put ours first. The cycle becomes complete by us doing the same for them.

Our generation of women is unique for many reasons. Although we were nurtured and supported allegedly unchangeable moral codes and ethics, our world rapidly changed.

We brought up our children in a much more lenient manner than we were raised. As educated adults we wanted the best for our progeny so we kept giving them more. Media exposed them to everything, and the world became very small. More than ever we find ourselves being responsible to both our parents and our children. Although my parents cannot relate to my children's values and visa versa, we have the belief systems from both.

With all this as our legacy, it is time for each of us to rediscover our power as midlife women. In truth, we have had a matriarchal society for centuries. Even though it seems to be a man's world, women have always been at the core and essence of success. Here is a little vignette to illustrate my point.

Stanley, the mayor, was walking down the street with his wife. Construction was taking place on a nearby building. A man's voice shouted down from the rooftop, "Helen! Helen! Look up. It's me, Ralph." The mayor's wife looked up and shouted back that it was nice to see him.

The mayor asked who the man on the roof was, and Helen replied that he had gone to high school with her. Smugly Stanley said, "Look how lucky you are, Helen. You could have been married to a construction worker rather than the mayor." Helen just smiled at him and said calmly, "Stanley, had I married Ralph, guess who the mayor would have been?"

Don't ever sell yourself short. Do you know how to spell guide, mentor, home base, safety zone and caretaker in one word? Authentic power is spelled:

WOMAN

Even Eagles Need a Push

David McNally in his book Even Eagles Need A Push has written the most poignant story that describes parenting.

The eagle gently coaxed her offspring toward the edge of the nest. Her heart quivered with conflicting emotions as she felt their resistance to her persistent nudging. "Why does the thrill of soaring have to begin with the fear of falling?" she thought. This ageless question was still unanswered for her.

As in the tradition of the species, her nest was located high on the shelf of a sheer rock face. Below there was nothing but air to support the wings of each child. "Is it possible that this time it will not work?" she thought. Despite her fears, the eagle knew it was time. Her parental mission was all but complete. There remained one final task—the push.

The eagle drew courage from an innate wisdom. Until her children discovered their wings, there was no purpose for their lives. Until they learned how to soar, they would fail to understand the privilege it was to have been born an eagle. The push was the greatest gift she had to offer. It was her supreme act of love. And so one by one she pushed them, and they flew!

As women, mothers, or wives, we can relate to this story. We have been there, done that. It is our nature to make things easier for others. At this stage in life we have the communication skills, the experiences, the knowledge and the ability to teach others what we know—and then to set them free to choose what, how and when to use those skills. Only when they are independent and fly themselves will those under our wings grow and learn. Coaxing others to that edge and pushing them to fly is a noble mission—and one worth choosing. We are, after all, a product of our choices, not our circumstances.

> Now it is your turn to choose.
> Choose to peek over the edge of the cliff.
> Choose to be nudged by this book. Choose to fly!

The Wisdom of Eleanor Roosevelt

1. You must do the thing you think you cannot do.
2. Life was meant to be lived, and curiosity must be kept alive. One must never, for whatever reason, turn his back on life.
3. You gain strength, courage and confidence by every experience in which you really stop to look fear in the face.
4. No one can make you feel inferior without your consent.
5. You get more joy out of the giving to others, and should put a good deal of thought into the happiness you are able to give.
6. You learn by living.
7. It is not fair to ask of others what you are unwilling to do yourself.
8. When you cease to make a contribution, you begin to die.
9. About the only value the story of my life may have is to show that one can, even without any particular gifts, overcome obstacles that seem insurmountable if one is willing to face the fact that they must be overcome.

THINGS MY MOTHER TAUGHT ME

- My Mother taught me LOGIC… "If you fall off that swing and break your neck, you can't go to the store with me."
- My Mother taught me MEDICINE… "If you don't stop crossing your eyes, they're going to freeze that way."
- My Mother taught me TO THINK AHEAD… "If you don't pass your spelling test, you'll never get a good job!"
- My Mother taught me ESP… "Put your sweater on; don't you think that I know when you're cold?"
- My Mother taught me TO MEET A CHALLENGE… "What were you thinking? Answer me when I talk to you… Don't talk back to me!"
- My Mother taught me HUMOR… "When that lawn mower cuts off your toes, don't come running to me."
- My Mother taught me how to BECOME AN ADULT… "If you don't eat your vegetables, you'll never grow up."
- My mother taught me ABOUT SEX… "How do you think you got here?"
- My mother taught me about GENETICS… "You are just like your father!"
- My mother taught me about my ROOTS… "Do you think you were born in a barn?"
- My mother taught me about the WISDOM of AGE… "When you get to be my age, you will understand."
- My mother taught me about ANTICIPATION… "Just wait until your father gets home."
- My mother taught me about RECEIVING… You are going to get it when we get home.
- And my all time favorite thing—JUSTICE "One day you will have kids, and I hope they turn out just like YOU—then you'll see what it's like."

CHAPTER THREE

THE EMOTIONAL ROLLER COASTER

We feel most upset when we respond to criticism or resentment with guilt and fear. A natural response is to assign blame for our discomfort. Self-approval and self-acceptance lead us to positive change while blame is one sure way to stay in a problem. By blaming either ourselves or someone else, we give away our power to understand what is really happening. Recognizing more about the situation and why we take the victim's role enables us to rise above conflict and take control.

Almost invariably our parents taught us the same beliefs they were taught, and we still hold on to them whether they benefit us or not. Even as adults, we often keep trying to please our parents—or our parents' wishes even if they are no longer alive.

> *We are a product of our choices, not of our circumstances!*
> *Circumstances do not determine people, they reveal them!*

How and what you think determines how you will perceive the world and your place in it. Thoughts are more than conclusions; they serve as drivers, filters and magnets for your experiences. Since you are the only person using your mind, you may think whatever you choose. You create your reality by selecting and interpreting input from the outside world that backs up your belief system. Questions of accurate interpretation of reality become irrelevant since we each consider ourselves to be seeing things as they are, even though we are only seeing them from our point of view. Our thoughts and beliefs, therefore, are more than conclusions; they are the prime causative factors of all our future experiences.

Stop for a moment and catch your thoughts. What are you thinking right now? Since your thoughts shape how you experience life, is what and how you are thinking now what you want to become true for you? Many times you operate on autopilot and are totally unaware of your thought processes, but every thought determines how you behave and how you act and react with the world. Therefore, increased inner awareness equals outer effectiveness.

Exercise: CLICHÉS AND OTHER EXPRESSIONS

The purpose of this exercise is to become more aware of thought patterns you may use unconsciously. Do you use any of these expressions? Can you think of a better ways to express these feelings?

- I cried my eyes out.
- It blew my mind.
- I feel stuffed.
- I froze with terror.
- I went crazy.
- I flipped out.
- I fight for: attention, what I believe in, for my rights.
- I am: torn apart, eaten up with anger, heart broken, dead on my feet, not good enough, at the boiling point, sick to death, spaced out.
- I got cold feet.
- I'm dying: to retire, to get that, to see that.
- There is a knot in my stomach.
- My feet are killing me.
- It gives me a pain in the neck, tears my guts apart, sets my teeth on edge, makes my skin crawl, rips me apart, makes my blood boil.
- My heart is broken.
- My mind is blank.

Exercise: Uncovering Widely Held Beliefs

Which of the following statements do you accept or use? They could affect how you see the world without you realizing it. What your mind believes, your body will achieve. Are these the self-fulfilling prophecies you wish to create?

Health-related beliefs

- Old age brings illness.
- Only the good die young.
- Cancer, stroke, or heart disease causes death.
- Without medicine disease can't improve.
- I'll die at the same age as my parents.
- No pain no gain.
- Ignorance is bliss.
- What you don't know can't hurt you.

Relationship beliefs

- Being competitive brings out the best in us. Being cooperative is being a wimp.
- Women are better at—
- Men are better at—
- Good guys finish last.

Prosperity and work beliefs

- Money is power.
- What goes around, comes around.
- It is a no-win situation.
- I'll be the first one laid off.
- It always happens to me.

Words that wound and words that heal

- Knock 'em dead.
- Read it and weep.

- You are: not good enough, too good, a walking time bomb, a jerk, so kind, a glutton for punishment, too hard on yourself, good as gold, so beautiful, smart as a whip, thick-skinned, thin-skinned, a sight for sore eyes.
- Be careful or: you will fall, catch cold, become the next victim, get sick.

Some positive statements you may want to implant

- I love myself no matter what!
- My body is a safe, comfortable and pleasurable place to be.
- I deserve relationships that are fun, easy and supportive.
- I am enough, I have enough, and I do enough.
- I now reclaim all my personal power.
- I have everything I need to get everything I want.

* * *

Your perceptions alert you to new possibilities and potentials, yet they can also trigger old responses. Every thought is either directly beneficial or it creates additional challenges for you. Since there are no neutral thoughts, stay away from patterns of thought that lead to problems and pain. Since how we think determines how we act, if we struggle with a difficult or unresolvable problem, our stalemate is usually not the result of what we are doing about the problem but how we are thinking about it. This means that it is more beneficial to understand the root cause of a problem—why it is there—than to treat the symptoms.

Often we respond as adults the way we responded as children. To become real adults, we need to examine and clearly evaluate the patterns set up in our early lives—and accept or reject elements of those patterns as fitting or unfitting to the adult life we want. This is the only way to appropriate action that will produce happiness, satisfaction and success.

The Emotional Roller Coaster 53

Too often conflicts are blown out of proportion according to our emotional needs of the moment. Many of these needs stem from issues that have not been resolved in the past, and they keep coming back to us like a ringing phone or snooze alarm. In these flashback moments we may still view situations through the memories of our childhood rather than think and act as the adult we have become. We can learn not to reenact childhood patterns of behavior in adult life. We can notice if our emotional reactions are appropriate to the situation or if we are merely throwing an adult tantrum. Until we have gotten good at recognizing our thinking patterns, we may experience chameleonlike shifts in logic and thinking in daily living as basic assumptions change between behaving like a child and like an adult.

Whenever you need to reconfirm your adult role, look into a mirror and say positive things to yourself. Remind yourself of how you have effectively changed. You are a grownup expected to make responsible decisions, not a child afraid of being scolded for making a wrong one. Notice that other people often criticize only what we acknowledge to them as our shortcomings. Therefore, when we *own* our inadequacies, we give other people permission to reinforce them. We give power to what we believe about ourselves, both good and bad. Thoughts are only word forms strung together to carry the meanings we choose to give them. Doesn't it make sense to think thoughts that nourish and support us?

Equally important is learning how to have emotions that serve us instead of driving us uncontrollably. Changing our emotions can change our thinking and behaviors. This, in turn, creates different, more beneficial outcomes in our lives. To become sensitized to the full spectrum of your emotions, notice and label what and how you feel (good, bad, frustrated, disappointed, angry, disturbed, bored). Many times we are unaware when we feel good and only notice when we feel bad. Here is an exercise to help you expand the understanding of your range of emotions.

Exercise: A Feel Good List

Make a list of 300 things you are grateful for:

- 100 things you have.
- 100 qualities you possess.
- 100 things you have done in your life.

Put this list on your bathroom mirror, and on your refrigerator. Scanning it is a great pick-me-up. You get a chance to realize what a treasure chest your life is.

* * *

Questioning the underlying patterns of personal dissatisfaction and discovering what is limiting our achievements are more efficient than looking for answers to specific problems. Deep questioning gets us to the root causes rather than the symptoms. What we learn also influences the way we think and work, the quality of our lives and our definition of success and happiness. Education can help us make better choices in our lives if it is coupled with experience can we develop the wisdom to stabilize our lives and recognize our paths to satisfaction.

So many times we repeat old patterns hoping for different results, however, without new approaches, the outcomes will be the same as in the past. With the development of more effective insights, we can speed our learning through experience and quickly convert what we learn into new applications. In midlife, we have a wealth of resources to draw upon.

Les Brown, the great motivator, says, "Each of us has something good to offer. We must learn to balance fun with work, and freedom with responsibilities. When you pursue greatness, you are taking responsibility for your life. You are choosing to accept the consequences of your actions. You may not be able to control what life puts in your path, but you can control who you are."

Fear drives us back into the past to think and ultimately to act the same way we did before—and yet we expect different results. We tend to do this because those are familiar thoughts that once may have worked, and they still feel comfortable to us—like a security blanket. Stretching our boundaries allows us to break the hold from the inhibiting and self-limiting influences of the past.

> *Live your dreams, not your past.*
> *Problems are only opportunities in disguise.*
> *Our emotions are signals.*
> *They are our red, yellow and green lights.*

Using emotions as feedback is a quick way of knowing what is or is not working for us. When feelings are suppressed and not expressed or acknowledged, they can erupt and intensify. When overwhelming changes occur, we often hold on to the uncomfortable feeling rather than releasing it and moving on.

Make conscious notes as to what situations, people, events or places trigger changes in your disposition. You can then mentally visualize yourself back in the experience while creating the emotion you desire as vividly and compellingly as possible. This anchoring technique self-programs your mind positively. The visualization pairs the stimulus over which you have no control with the emotional state to which you would like to anchor. The next time you are in that experience, the desired emotion is automatically accessed.

Too often we worry about a future that may never happen. This worry may pervade our thoughts about making a living, making the most of life with the least effort or any of a vast multitude of haunting *what ifs*. Many of us are not happy with our lives. We wake up tired after sleep and go on to the next day knowing that the routine of that day will be exactly like that of the previous one. In spite of the fact that in this midlife cycle of life we can become more individuated and self-directed than society generally accepts as the norm, some of us worry so much that we may never attain anywhere near our potential.

As an example, consider these two apple seeds. One seed thinks it must become a sprout—and does. The sprout then becomes a sapling, and the sapling becomes a young tree. Several years later, it produces its first crop of luscious apples. The second seed never thinks about the first step. It is too busy worrying about whether it's apples will be red or yellow, juicy or tart, and how much fruit it will produce before it has even considered setting roots. This seed's thinking is wasting energy. Instead of living in the present, it is worrying about a future it cannot control. Of course, seeds just *do*, but if these seeds had been people, one would have become a strong tree, and the other would not have gotten out of the ground.

Instead of worrying, which really solves nothing, visualize a movie screen in front of you and run the events of the day. If any negative aspects show up, stop the movie and see how the negatives could be transformed into positives. Then run the movie again with your new improved version. It won't change the past, but it will help you be more objective in your perspective of the day. The reward is that your transmuted feelings now will be acting positively on what you consider negative acts.

> *Fear and worry are interest paid in advance on something you may never own. Why bother?*

Exercise: An Integrity Checklist

A quick way to assess what is and isn't balanced in your life is to make an integration list heading the major areas you consider important such as: relationships, work, home, health, friends, etc. Put each heading at the top of a column. Under each heading, list any number of topics that apply to the heading in your life. For example, under relationships you may have categories such as spouse, lover, children, parents, etc. Rate how well you feel you are doing in each topic area on a scale of 1 to 10 with a 1 being the weakest and a 10 being the strongest. As you assess each area, see what needs attention, figure out why and recommit to improve it.

Take a deep breath, relax and know that life never gives you more than you can handle. Here is a variation of the checklist you can try.

List the major areas of your life:

- Relationships: Are you telling the truth, loving yourself and respecting others?
- Work: Are you making a contribution to the best of your ability. Are you receiving the money you deserve? Are you at the right job?
- Home: Are you taking care of your body with respect to nutrition and exercise?

Add to your integrity check list and consult it daily. Make it your intention to recommit to doing what makes you feel good.

* * *

A comforting feeling is the conviction that you are coping even when you think you can't. Remember that your heart is beating, you are breathing and your nervous system is functioning whether you think about it or not. Your conviction of confidence can become just as automatic.

To experience your feelings and learn more about yourself, notice your trigger situations—what gets you stressed, what makes you happy, what makes you feel content. Knowing what is going on will help you stop runaway dysfunctional feelings before they start and reach peace and contentment on command. When you integrate and control these feelings, you become a more healthy adult, not just a functioning grown-up.

Forgiveness is also a powerful cleanser. Many of us have experienced what it is like to be hurt emotionally. Our lives are littered with *should haves, if onlys* and *might have beens*. This often happens when we harbor resentment toward a friend or a lover, but failures in self-forgiveness are usually the toughest to get through. This emotional garbage plugs our hearts and minds and plagues us with anxiety and guilt.

You can unblock this potent energy and get back to being more loving, flexible and understanding by just being forgiving. Here is a technique that can help you get started. Get into a comfortably warm bath (with bubbles, oils or scents makes it even more special) and just soak in the cocoon you have created. Play some soothing music, dim the lights and feel the tension leave your body and mind. Envision your resentment as a dirty film on your body. As you soak, see the film of your resentment, anger and shame dissolve and settle like a sediment of fine, black soil. Gather the soil of your resentment, put it in a beautiful pot of your imagining and plant a flower in it. Watch the flower grow and bloom—and smile at its beauty. As you let the water out of the tub, send the remaining scraps of your resentment, anger, and bitterness down the drain—and feel renewed and refreshed. This is a wonderful ritual to practice on a daily basis as nothing negative gets a chance to build up. Feeling "drained" can be fine in these instances.

Another way to gain inner peace is to clearly define the new way you want to live. If you do not, you will continue to respond to old attractions and then blame yourself for not becoming the person you want to be. Thinking such thoughts as "I hate myself for being like that," or How could I be so dumb?" create a negative and self-destructive mental environment as well as a lack of love and respect for yourself. Life's lessons can be learned without beating yourself up. Recognize that no one can love you more than you love yourself. If you don't put yourself as first in line to receive your own love and respect, why should anyone else love or respect you?

Create a self-esteem profile. List all your qualities both positive and negative. Assess these on a 1 to 10 scale, the same way you did the integration scale. Use 1 as needing the most improvement and 10 for being terrific. Then analyze what you have to do to change what you consider the negatives into positives. Self-acceptance is the first step to self-esteem, and that leads to self-respect. We are usually too hard on ourselves and emphasize the negatives instead of the positives. If we have one hundred things to do and two aren't done correctly, we usually remember what is not correct and berate ourselves while not giving ourselves credit for all the wonderful things we did accomplish. In the same vein, when we look in the mirror, we focus on what we don't like about ourselves (the wrinkles, the extra pounds) rather than see the beauty of what is and the rest as imperfections that we would like to improve.

This following exercise is another variation of the self-esteem profile. Doing both can bring forth different observations. Although I am giving you various lists, each one has its own value, and different insights can result to help you facilitate the changes you may want for fun and growth.

Exercise: A Self-Esteem Profile

At the top of a piece of paper write the following statement: "What I am is—" and list all the qualities, positive and negative, you associate with yourself. Fill up the entire page, free-associating, not worrying about whether they are true or not. When you are done, underline all those characteristics you consider positive. You are looking at a profile of the current state of your self-esteem. The *negative* qualities are those things you want to forgive yourself for, or reverse through implanting new thoughts.

Take out another clean sheet of paper. Write at the top: "The things I want to acknowledge myself for are—" and make a list of at least 25 things for which you are approve of in yourself. Give yourself permission to sing your own praises. Saying *no* to what you don't want opens the door to what you do want. Remember; whatever you have created in the past can be changed in the present and future. You deserve to take charge of your life and create whatever you wish. Your past does not need to continue into the future unless you want it to.

Next, make a list of ten ways to increase your pleasure and aliveness. Schedule them into your daily routine to add more fun and youthfulness to your life.

* * *

Even though we may do the best we know how, sometimes we have to fall apart to get ourselves really together. If our lives feel like they are going smoothly, we seldom seek change. It is only in the midst of confusion, turmoil, chaos or pain that we attempt new directions for different results. Notice how we respond to what is happening inside, not to what is actually going on outside when we make a decision. When everything is going the way we want and we get the desired results, although there seems to be no need for change, use this time of tranquility as an opportunity to learn something new.

The way to create a positive mentality is to self-nurture by making a commitment of compassion and love to yourself. Strive to see the positive by encouraging and accepting yourself as a loving parent or as best friend would. We each need to activate and strengthen this inner nurturing voice. If we don't know how to give ourselves approval, we beg for that approval from everyone else. Our nurturing voice is an incredible comfort. She can make the hardest times and the greatest challenges easier. This nurturing voice is invaluable any time you need a pat on the back, a dose of warm love or an energy boost.

To get the balance that you want in your life, take a step back and ask, "How important are those *gottas* and *haftas*?" Figure out what you want in your life by eliminating what you don't want. See what is remaining and just add more "goodies."

An easy way to instantaneously know what and whom you want in your life is to make a list of what you would do if you had six months to live in perfect health. Toxic people and situations become immediately apparent. Do this now. You just may be amazed at your results.

Take a close look at the list you made as it represents the things in life that you presently value the most. This will give you a clearer perspective as to what you are doing, how you are living and how you wish to live. By eliminating people, activities and situations that do not help you move toward your purposes, your life will have room to include more of what makes you alive and content.

STRATEGIES FOR CHANGING YOUR MOOD

1. Look at the funny side of a serious situation. By making light of a heavy predicament, we immediately de-escalate it. Visually blow it totally out of proportion until it becomes absurd.
2. Look for the positive aspects of the situation instead of only the negatives. Focus on learning something about how you can respond and grow from it and then move on.
3. Solve problems creatively. In this way you are more likely to dissipate the problem than escalate it.
4. Pursue a goal. Reestablish your dreams and work toward them.
5. Take time out to play. Then come back and view the situation. Our attitude changes when we feel better and can view the situation more objectively.
6. Use relaxation techniques such as guided imagery, yoga, t'ai chi or deep breathing.

Using any combination of these techniques will put our lives back into perspective. A true sign of burnout is exaggerating our dilemmas. These strategies are sure to shrink things back to normal size.

Stresses and crisis are in everyone's life. When we are in balance we don't lose our perspective, and it becomes easy to keep things in proportion. Prioritizing is then a natural process, and we are more likely to be sociable and creative. When we are balanced, we have high self-esteem and a can-do attitude—and nothing seems overwhelming.

The future arrives one hour at a time. Go one step and one day at a time focusing on the present moment. With these strategies, balance becomes a way of life.

Happiness is a direction, not a destination.

Aging

Do you realize that the only time in our lives when we like to get old is when we're kids? If you're less than ten years old, you're so excited about aging that you think in fractions.

"How old are you?" "I'm four and a half."

You're never 36 and a half, but you're four and a half going on five! That's the key. You get into your teens, now they can't hold you back.

You jump to the next number.

"How old are you?" "I'm gonna be 16."

You could be 12, but you're gonna be 16. And then the greatest day of your life happens: you become 21. Even the words sounds like a ceremony—you BECOME 21. YES!

But then you turn 30. Ooohhh, what happened here? Makes you sound like bad milk. He TURNED. We had to throw him out. There's no fun now.

What's wrong? What changed?

You BECOME 21, you TURN 30, then you're PUSHING 40...stay over there, it's all slipping away...

You BECOME 21, you TURN 30, you're PUSHING 40, you REACH 50...my dreams are gone...

You BECOME 21, you TURN 30, you're PUSHING 40, you REACH 50 and then you MAKE IT to 60... Whew! I didn't think I'd make it.

You BECOME 21, you TURN 30, You're PUSHING 40, you REACH 50, you MAKEIT to 60, and by then you've built up so much speed, you HIT 70!

After that, it's a day by day thing. You HIT Wednesday, you get into your 80s, you HIT lunch. I mean my grandmother won't even buy green bananas, "Well it's an investment, you know, and maybe a bad one."

And it doesn't end there. Into the 90's, you start going backwards: I was JUST 92. Then a strange thing happens, if you make it over 100, you become a little kid again: I'm 100 and a half!!

Age is a funny thing.

Personal Mapmaking

Roy Hughes Roberts

The process of Chapter Three has been to take you through many ways to examine how you look at yourself so that you can see more clearly, avoid unnecessary stress and live a happier life. In the next section, Roy Roberts helps you look at making and using maps of your life to assist you as you make your way from the person you are now to the person you want to become.

Dr. R. Hughes Roberts, has authored "HOW... Observations by a Traveler" and numerous articles in the field of human thought and action. As a counselor and professional mediator he has worked with individual clients, business professionals and prison inmate groups. He has presented independently developed course work through University or Maryland, Boise State University and Northwest Nazarene College. You may contact him via email: strebor@cyberhighway.net.

We relate to the world by creating mental images. These images might be the memory of your mother's face, or the scent of a high school sweetheart's perfume. They might also be more like a script or scenario that describes how you expect important parts of the external world to respond in a specific situation. For instance, as you drive home, you may visualize your father becoming angry as you tell him you had an accident with his new car. These mental scripts can also describe things like the *if-then* nature of physical reality, *If* I fall off a tall building, *then* I will be hurt or die. Mental images or created scripts about the physical world reflect how an individual believes the world or the people in it exist and act.

Beliefs are very strong influences in each of our lives; but, since beliefs are made of mental images that we create, just because we believe something is so does not make it so. Much like maps, our mental images or beliefs represent something that we can't really *know* directly or in its entirety. We might then refer to these mental representations as *maps* of our reality.

Maps have two important characteristics. The first is that they are representational: they are not the actual thing mapped. Depending on which aspect is being mapped, maps of the same territory can look remarkably different. In other words, a weather map of the United States will look remarkably different from a road map or a topographic map, even though the place mapped is the same. The second characteristic of maps is their accuracy. This could involve things such as when the map was made or the level of detail the mapmaker used. For example, a road map of the entire country would probably be of little value in helping you find your friend in a suburb of Cleveland. A weather map from last year would not help you plan this year's picnic.

Our mental maps are much the same. We begin with a collection of information—mental images—and we put them together as the relational or cause-and-effect structures we have selected to represent as our reality. How well our mental maps help us navigate through life depends on whether we are applying the right kind of map to the problem and whether that map is accurate or current.

Driving down a road with a recent road atlas as your guide, you may find a new portion of a highway not shown on the map. In such an instance, you might find a sign that will tell you where that road leads. You may look at the representations of where the towns are located relative to each other on the map and make a good guess about where the uncharted road goes. As a result, you may get to where you are going by using outdated information and good guessing. Sometimes, however, you get lost.

If you have ever experienced any of these things in actual travel, you may have an appreciation for the value of a good map and will understand that maps don't necessarily represent all of the known the territory. They may be inaccurately drawn, they may be outdated or they may be complete fabrications and not represent the territory in any fashion. Some maps accurately represent a territory that does not exist in any reality. I have read a number of fictional books that provide maps of territories or worlds that exist only within the confines of the story. We know these maps are fictional because the cover of the book says *fiction*, but how do we determine when someone else's or our own mental maps are more fictional than realistic?

If you have done any traveling you probably understand that maps are only a suggestion of roads and towns and their relationship with each other. Maps also suggest other kinds of relationships or structures of things we find in the physical world. We can find maps that depict population concentrations, topography, temperature averages, rainfall or political boundaries. Sometimes what is depicted on a map does not meet our needs, so we find it of little or no value.

The elements included in the map, the accuracy and timeliness of the mapmaker, and the intention of the map user all combine to produce what may be called *structure*. When structure is similar between the map and what you experience in the world, then the map is useful.

How often do you encounter someone who goes about their daily life responding to things much differently than you? Their responses to living do not seem to correspond with your understanding of the situation. You may decide they have a different map of the territory, as their viewpoint is much different from yours. Will you consider them as crazy or wise, foolish or enlightened? After much consideration you may find their responses more to your liking, and adopt their map or viewpoint as your own. Perhaps you will discuss the situation with this other person, and both of you might adjust your maps.

We feel more comfortable (less stressed) when the maps we create correspond as closely as possible with what goes on in the world. Correspondence in this sense means predictability; that is, if we follow the directions for our thoughts and actions that we derive from the map, we will get where we expect to go. Information changes frequently, however, both from the world outside our skins and the world inside. The *truth* changes frequently over just one's lifetime. On the grand scale, relativity and quantum physics changed the way we see the universe. On a smaller scale, the pronouncements of nutritionists changed the way we look at bacon and eggs. In just this same manner, other kinds of information change, too. We need to incorporate these changes readily if we hope to be comfortable in a world of changing information and structure.

One way we do that is to have not one map, but several. This way, when new information presents itself, we can make a map that applies specifically to the new information as a special case. For example, we all know that the earth is roughly a sphere spinning on its axis and traveling around the sun. As we plan our road trip from Denver to New York, we use flat maps in our atlas, however. Denver is at a much higher elevation than New York, but our maps are smooth. We begin our trip at *sunrise* even though we know that, relative to the earth, the sun is standing still, and it is the earth that is moving and turning. When we get to New York, we may use a subway map that looks nothing like actual physical layout of the tracks, but helps us catch the right train to see the Statue of Liberty.

In the same way, we have internal maps that help us navigate through life. The first map we create is one called *me*. Then we make *mom*, then *dad*, then *world*. We expand our maps into *siblings, relatives, friends, lovers, the community, the workplace, the nation, the human race, science, politics, ethics, religion, my religion, my personal relationship with god*. The difficulty with having so many independent maps is that, first, it's hard to keep up to date with all the changes and, second, it may be difficult to know which map to use. Consider the many often conflicting maps you have to deal with when you interact with your aged mother who is more like a child than an adult.

How did you create those maps? What are the elements of these maps? Do you insist that the information on your maps stands up to some validation? How do you use them in your daily life? What provisions have you made to compare and update your maps? The generalizations we make about the structure of the world and the events we encounter determine how we make, interpret and use our maps.

Each person shapes his or her maps, models or viewpoints in a unique way. Take a look around your world today. Examine the representations (maps) you use in relating to your spouse/lover, friends, children, peers, strangers, and people of different religious, political or ethnic heritage. Do your maps allow for individual differences or are they generalizations that you expect to apply to all situations? Do you make derogatory comments about *men! women!* or *kids!*—or persons of different races, religions or political persuasions. These kinds of comments usually come from people who are convinced that their map *is* the territory (the truth of unprocessed reality).

You may notice here that you make sense of any situation through representations you make of people, places and events. These become the sensations you experience within your body/brain. Visual information, for example, is carried by light to your eyes, through your optic nerve and into your visual cortex where your brain interprets it. This interpreted information is actually what you *see*—not the light from outside. Most of the brain's activity is directed toward filtering out unwanted or unnecessary sensory information so that the processing center is not swamped with too much conflicting or confusing input. As a result, no one's map is completely accurate—nor is it completely like anyone else's map.

You can gain a great deal of power over your world by taking responsibility for your maps and, consequently, the ways you respond to your world and the people in it. You might find that only *you* can be held responsible for your happiness or sadness or anger or joy. Phrases like "You make me mad" or "I want someone to make me happy" simply won't make sense any longer. In order to take this responsibility you may find it necessary to do some things differently.

The first thing you must do is to treat map making as an ongoing process. One way to stay young is to constantly update your maps, cleaning the outdated ones from your mental closet. Too often, as adults we rely on maps that were meant for children—maps that were designed to protect us, not to spur us to grow to our maximum potential. Too often, we follow our family's traditional atlas without testing or validation.

You have probably heard someone say that it is good to live *in the moment*. That means to experience life without the judgments, labels and expectations that you bring from the past. You may find it helpful to change how you perceive your day. Instead of a routine, which is disturbing if interrupted, you may want to think of your day as unfolding before you in a process of dynamic change from which you can grow.

To change your thinking and perceive various experiences differently, you might ask yourself the following questions: Do I require the people around me to respond to a rigid protocol? Do I expect them to act according to a script I've written for them? Do I define the people and events that I encounter in terms of purpose or meaning? Do I search endlessly for *who I am*? Do I find myself upset because I've done something *not like me*? Or do my maps include provisions for moment-by-moment differences in a dynamic world of change around me? Do I allow the people within my world to be expressive, open and dynamic—in short, changeable?

The way you answer those questions says something about the way you have constructed your maps of reality. What will you do about your process of map making and map using? When will you start? How about now?

> *Just when I was getting used to yesterday, along came today.*

Chapter Four

Breaking the Stress Barrier

Cooked, burned, whipped, and beaten

We all know what it feels like to get emotionally mangled by the weight of the day's struggles. The problem is not the external circumstances; but rather how we perceive and then react to it. For example, I love horseback riding and find it thrilling. That experience may create abject fear (super stress) in someone else. Stress that motivates us, called eustress, is beneficial; paralyzing stress definitely is not. In general, situations that are perceived as low to moderate stress are felt as energizing; situations of moderate to high stress are felt as debilitating. That *moderate* point differs from individual to individual. People seldom experience the same degree of stress in a given circumstance. This reemphasizes the fact that stress is inside of us, not outside of us. With this knowledge, we can choose to view many of the problems that we encounter as discomfort and stress or as a challenge and excitement.

To shift your perspective in the midst of uncomfortable stress, visualize a personal success, a past achievement or an energizing vacation that will create a positive feeling. Induce relaxation and peace. Actually leaving the stressful environment for a few moments and taking several deep breaths allows the autonomic nervous system (brain waves, heart rate, blood pressure) to slow down.

Exercise: Time Out

This exercise is to give you some still time. Sit quietly or walk alone and simply listen to your thoughts, interact with them, notice the feelings they bring.

Doing this on a daily basis allows you time to be centered. You don't have to come to any conclusions—just be here now with your thoughts and emotions. This will help you with your decisions of the day, whether they are big or small. It will allow you to become clearer about what you want to do, prevent knee-jerk reactions, and help you make better choices.

Inserting little periods of silence between important moments of your life will help keep you from operating on autopilot and put you back into a proactive position. This process just may reveal alternatives that you would have missed otherwise.

Imagine yourself as peaceful, courageous and resourceful, to invite these qualities to become part of your life. These qualities do not arise from the events you face; they come from your imagery—and your imagery determines how you deal with the events.

* * *

Everybody Has a Body

There are also things you can do to prepare your body for emotional stress. An ongoing exercise program will build stamina and help you rid yourself of tension when it hits. Get your body in good working order and establish or reestablish healthful eating and exercise habits. Consume foods that are low in fat, salt and sugar and high in complex carbohydrates. Fruits, vegetables, whole grains, pasta, potatoes and plenty of water are good ideas. If you are physically able, exercise for at least thirty minutes, three times a week. Balance your day of mental work or routine activity with exercise. If you feel fatigued, take a short relaxing walk. Always remember the word *balance*, however. Too much of a good thing might be harmful. You might be overdoing your exercise program if you are very tired and your legs feel heavy all the time. Don't exercise vigorously when you are sick because your body needs its energy to fight exhaustion and infection.

There are also exercise programs to get your psyche in shape. Listening to relaxation tapes or meditating creates a state that is the opposite of tension. Meditating regularly gives you a facility for easing into calmness that you can bring to other situations. As an additional part of your life, having the right music in the background is a great tool to relax or to inspire you.

If your internal world is chaotic, your interaction with the outside world around you will reflect that chaos. Do you seem to get out of bed every morning and go through your daily routine mechanically? Are sex and other enjoyments only distant memories? As this day ends, do you have nothing to look forward to but duplicating the same day tomorrow? Prior to fixing the world (spouse, house, friends, job), you need to get your inner self in working order. This will give you energy, stamina and enthusiasm to get on with the outer work.

> *God grant me the senility to forget the people I never liked anyway, the good fortune to run into the ones I do, and the eyesight to tell the difference.*

Exercise: ENERGY BOOSTERS

To charge yourself as you start each day, here is a great way to begin. Upon waking, review the day that lies before you, imagining it to be as positive and beneficial as it could possibly be. Imagine fun breaks as well as the healthy lifestyle habits that you would like to acquire. As you visualize your day, see others responding to you in supportive ways. When you imagine others reacting positively to you, they very often do end up behaving that way. You may not have been aware that your body language and other subconscious forms of communication were contributing to their previously negative reactions.

If you tend to fall back to sleep while doing this exercise, try gently getting out of bed. Either sit in a chair or begin your morning routine while you do your imagining. Breathe deeply during this time. Soft music is also helpful to maintain a relaxing state of mind. Some people report that a warm morning shower is excellent for their morning imaging of their peaceful day. Waking up in this manner subdues the chaos within you.

Exercise: END OF THE DAY

At the close of the day, as you are drifting into sleep, mentally review the day. Focus on the positive events. If you come to a memory of something you don't feel was your best effort, skip over it. Celebrate all your positive experiences first. Next, allow your mind to consider any negative events, but this time imagine them as you wish they had happened. This provides a mental rehearsal for the next time the opportunity arises.

As you go through this process, be careful not to be judgmental or to revive whatever harmful emotions you might have felt during the day. Emotions felt while remembering something add power by imprinting themselves on all similar events. If you think about failing to win a new account, for example, and you let yourself feel self-anger or resentment or a drop in confidence, you have just imprinted an expectation of these emotions on the accompanying behavior. Change your thinking to reflect how you would like to act or react the next time this situation occurs. Now you have imbedded positive seeds of thought and emotion that will arise naturally the next time you are in that scenario.

Take time out and nurture yourself. Without self-nurturing, your life will become a series of monotonous and stressful days. Before you burn out, take time off and enjoy what makes you happy. Relaxation is not a treat; it is a necessity for your physical and emotional health. A good coach knows the importance of resting the players now and then.

Remember that this is *your* life. Are you doing what you want? Are you getting what you need? Are you loving and caring for yourself? Ultimately, before you can take care of someone else, you must first take care of yourself.

* * *

Living with Compromise

Everything in life is a compromise. This means that everything has positive aspects as well as negative ones. Going on a vacation is great; yet it is expensive, and you could be saving that money for tomorrow. Marriage is wonderful, but now you have another person's schedule and moods to accommodate. Becoming a parent is super; on the other hand, it takes a lot of energy, limits your time and brings added responsibility. Again, how you think, act and respond to the situation is what counts. If you understand that any choice means accepting a compromise, then stress is not as much an issue because you understand that the positive and negative aspects of situations come as a package.

Since life is a series of compromises between what you want and what actually materializes, the skill that is most valuable to navigate through life serenely is *balance*. Start balancing by looking on the bright side of the current situations. For example, having more to do than you can possibly get done keeps you alive, growing and thriving. Think of it as job security.

For the balance that you want in life, take a step back and view your day as if you were a character in a drama. Now you are better able to write the next scene or the next act before you get back *into character*.

Stress and burnout are cracks and slippage in the building blocks of your balance. The cracks build slowly until the walls and foundation of your life start to erode and crumble with the symptoms of stress. Instead of actual hairline cracks that get steadily longer and wider, you start to feeling the symptoms of muscle tension, backache, headache, gastrointestinal distress, colds and allergies, skin rashes, hair loss, acne and so on. Just as with home maintenance, if you ignore those emotional cracks or just cover them up, you may wake up one morning to find half your life falling away into the backyard.

Cracks in Your Foundation

Many factors can be crack starters in our lives, from how we eat to how we exercise. Here are a few culprits that are best to avoid:

1. *Junk Food Diets:* The high salt and sugar content of junk foods makes us even more anxious and irritable and creates a higher risk for heart disease.
2. *Exercise Abuse:* Over exercising can be almost as much of a problem as under exercising. If you are in doubt, have an exercise physiologist or trainer give you a proper program that is beneficial for your needs.
3. *Bad Posture:* Since our spines must be vertical for the maximum amount of fresh oxygen to come in and carbon dioxide to go out, working slumped over a desk for hours builds up more stress, because we use only a third of our lung capacity in that position. Carbon dioxide gets trapped inside, and we can feel exhausted, lightheaded and nauseated.
4. *Sleep Deprivation:* The only time our cells totally regenerate are when we sleep. If we don't get enough sleep, we will be physically and emotionally stressed.
5. *Fluorescent Lights:* Working under such lights deplete our store of vitamin C, potassium and magnesium. Most corporations have noticed this and have changed to full-spectrum lighting.
6. *Air Conditioning and Heat:* Both dehydrate us. We may also be breathing the same stale air along with circulated impurities such as fumes from the copy machine or second hand smoke. Spend some time outside.
7. *Noise Pollution:* Noise from printers, telephones, refrigerators, radios and even nearby chatter can fray our nervous system. Sometimes people play loud, raucous music to help them forget the monotony of their jobs. Then they wonder why they can't relax. Envelop yourself in relative quietness if you can.
8. *Rushing Everywhere:* Because we live in a world that expects it *now*, we often make well-intentioned but dysfunctional choices to help us deliver on time. In other

words, haste makes waste. Get back into balance, and tasks develop their own flow and become naturally easier to perform.

> *Dear God,*
> *So far today, I have been innocent.*
> *I have not gossiped.*
> *I have not lost my temper.*
> *I have not been greedy, grumpy, nasty, selfish, proud or self-indulgent.*
> *I am very thankful for that—*
> *But in a few minutes, God, I'm going to get out of bed.*

Look at Your Little List

How important are those *gottas* and *haftas*? Take a step back from your life and view it objectively. Remember the list you made of what you would do if you had six months to live in perfect health. (If you skipped over that exercise, do it now!) Take a close look at this list because it represents the things in life that you value the most. Use it to put your life into perspective. How you are living, and how do you really wish to live? Are how you are living and how you wish to live congruent? If not, what do you have to add or eliminate to make the life you want a reality? A quick way to identify incongruities is by the use of metaphors.

* * *

Exercise: METAPHORS

Metaphors sometime make it easier to understand what is going on in our lives. To get yourself started, finish these sentences with a word or phrase:

My life is like a _____

My job is like a _____

My boss is like a _____

My relationship is like a _____

My health is like a _____

Add any other topic you want. At a glance you will immediately get feedback as to how you feel about each area and what needs more attention or change.

Another way to gain a different perspective on your life is to ask "just suppose" questions. "Just suppose I lived to be 100? Just suppose I had three million dollars? Just suppose money grew on trees? Just suppose I could live on the moon?" How would you answer these questions? How would it affect your thinking and your life if it were so? These types of questions might seem absurd, but they do generate a different point of view causing us to think and feel differently. See how many of these kind of questions you can come up with that are relevant to your life, and note what kinds of answers they generate.

* * *

Nurture yourself by taking time out to play. Working for hours and days on end tires the mind and dampens the soul. Take time out for fun as it will clear your mind, make your body feel better and awaken your soul to new possibilities. Then go back to work with renewed vigor. Some people need to *enforce* a balance of fun in their lives or they will forget to relax. If that sounds like you, keep a calendar of your fun activities alongside your work or *to do* activities. Mark the fun events in blue and the work activities in red. Is there balance, or is the fun end of your see-saw sitting on the ground. The red ink will tell you.

Stress and crises are in everyone's life, however, when you are in balance, you don't lose your perspective, and nothing seems overwhelming. A good sign of impending burnout is exaggerating your dilemmas. Taking things too seriously should be seen as a red flag. Burnout can be a *crash-and-burn* complete collapse. Sometimes people rise from the ashes much stronger than before the crash, but burnout can be a painful way to find your balance.

The Bright Side of Life

Uncontrolled escalating stress is what leads to burnout. As stress mounts, it can feel like a painful psychological swelling. Laughter is one of the best ways to deflate it. Look at the funny side of serious situations. By making light of a heavy predicament, you immediately depressurize it. Blow it all out of proportion until it becomes absurd and funny, and the pressurized situation seems to pop of its own accord. Humor takes practice, however. You cannot be funny under big pressure if you haven't practiced making light of little pressure. As an example, before you get aggravated when you are stuck in a traffic jam, think of yourself still there until you are old and gray. Think of the new service industries you could develop for meeting the needs of people eternally stuck in traffic—fly-in food and beverage services, 5 m.p.h. Stop & Go PortaPottys, or rickshaw emergency transportation. As the prospects make the scene ridiculous, stress evaporates—and you get a chance to develop your humor muscles for the really big jobs.

Whatever elements of this stress reduction package you choose to employ, remember to go one step and one day at a time. Use your imagination. (Imagination can make the difference between just being and being marvelous.) Focus on what is before you *now*. With these strategies, train and condition yourself so that balance becomes a way of life.

VITALITY

Is there a way for us to maintain, or regain, much of the vitality we had in our youth? *Yes!* Besides keeping a supple body and high metabolism, our behavior patters and attitudes contribute greatly to our energy levels.

When we watch children there are certain attributes that are common.

- They seek out things that are fun or find a way to have fun with what they are doing.
- They leave an activity when they feel bored or become more interested in something else.
- They are curious and usually eager to try anything at least once.
- They smile and laugh a lot.
- They openly express their emotions.
- They are creative and believe in the impossible.
- They are active.
- They are constantly growing mentally and physically.
- They will risk often and aren't afraid to fail.
- They learn enthusiastically.
- They generally don't worry or feel guilty
- They dream and vividly use their imagination.
- They are passionate.

Unfortunately, most of us learned to *act our age* as we grew up. A quick analysis can show how many of these characteristics fit your mode of behavior. If you discover a large disparity between your current personality and those of children, perhaps you have left behind some valuable energy traits of your youth. It is this energy that gives us the *high on life* feeling.

The traits of childhood and the judgment of adulthood can be effectively combined for our best interest. Childlike behavior encourages joy and creativity while adult perspective helps us maintain concern for the needs of others.

What stops you from awakening this childlike energy? Could it be that little voice inside that says, "What will my friends think?" "Grow up!" "You are making a fool of yourself!"? This is the part of you that expects you to accept any task and do it perfectly. Turn off that voice long enough to discover how much fun you can get by using your natural instincts for free, creative play and hobbies.

Since play and laughter are the things that go by the wayside when you are not feeling well. make a list of 40 things that are fun. Keep this list in an obvious place because, when you most need the boost, nothing sounds like fun. Fun enhances your immune system, your vital energy, your creativity and your will to live, and enables you to change perspective. Make yours a fun filled life. By changing your thoughts you change your future.

LIFE IS—

About who you love and who you hurt.

Who you make happy or unhappy purposefully.

About keeping or betraying trust.

About friendship, used as a sanctity or a weapon.

About what you say and mean, maybe hurtful, maybe heartening.

About starting rumors and contributing to petty gossip.

About what judgments you pass and why. And who your judgments are spread to.

About who you've ignored with full control and intention.

About jealousy, fear, ignorance and revenge.

About carrying inner hate and love, letting it grow, and spreading it.

But most of all, it's about using your life to touch or poison other people's hearts in such a way that could have never occurred alone.

Only you choose the way those hearts are affected, and those choices are what life is all about.

The Over-Committed, Over-Scheduled Woman

Susan Corbett

Susan Corbett, BA, CCLP, CTM, MCC, is president of Success Technologies, Inc. She specializes in business and personal coaching for small business owners, professionals, managers, and people in transition. She also develops and conducts courses for managers in corporations, including the Corporate Coaches Training Program. As part of the team that is Coach University, she worked to create what is now considered one of the premier coach-training programs in the world. She also helped to launch the International Coach Federation and remains on the Board of Directors. She has been awarded the Master Coach Certification from that organization. If you would like to contact Susan, her web site is http://www.coachcorbett.com; *her e-mail address is:* susan@coachcorbett.com.

Facing a life that feels out of control

When we were small children, we weren't able to take good care of ourselves. For about 18 years others cared for us. At the very time we were forming our core habits and beliefs on how to make it in the world, we were dependent on others to take care of us. We were also told that thinking about our own needs, wants and desires, was *selfish*, and we were not supposed to be *selfish*. On top of that, we added our perceptions that we are not skillful enough or good enough to be careful with ourselves. We can hear our mother's voice as we leave the house saying, "Be careful," as if without those constant reminders we would blindly destroy ourselves. It is no wonder, that as adults, we are not very good at self-care.

We did learn that one way to get cared for was to please our parents, achieve what they wanted for us, meet their expectations and imitate caring for others the way they did for us. Our parents were not bad people; they were just doing what they were taught by their parents. But since we were taught that thinking of ourselves was selfish, the way to get cared for was to take care of others first. This crippled us from learning to be responsible for our own self-care. Now as grown ups, we return to the childhood habits that seemed to work in the past. We strive to achieve more in our work. We adapt and accommodate to others. We give more to others. We fill others' needs before we fulfill our own. We focus on everything and everybody outside our selves.

We agree to do things and commit to activities, either because we think it will help others, or we think it will make us look good in somebody else's eyes, or maybe we'll even enjoy them. We don't even look to see how it fits in with what is truly important to us—our life's purpose. We even choose major life goals because we think we "should".

Thriving in your career while keeping a personal balance and perspective.

In my coaching practice, my clients often have many goals, many ideas and many plans. Part of my work is to encourage them to focus their energies on just a few. It's similar to gardening. After we plant the seeds, we watch the seedlings cluster together as they grow. If we leave them all in the ground, they will crowd each other out, and none of them will be healthy. If we thin them out, which initially may be a painful process for us, the result will be the healthy, growing plants we wanted.

Sometimes we may need help with thinning out our tasks and priorities. This means not only deciding what is most important, it also means being willing to put some things on a back burner. Some of the less important things can be postponed, rather than being permanently discarded as with the seedlings. Just as water, soil and sunlight are needed for healthy plants to grow, time, energy and other resources are needed for us to grow. And we cannot allow all of our dreams and plans to crowd into a limited amount of time and energy or none of the plans can materialize.

Are you so exhausted at the end of the day without enough time left over to take care of yourself or do the things you said you wanted to do? Many people need a personal tragedy or great illness in order to look at the way they prioritize their lives. For some people, a wake-up call comes in the form of a persistent inner voice that reminds them something is missing. Others may hear themselves repeat over and over again how they want to do something such as take a class, play the piano, play tennis.

Start by looking at what is truly important to you in the mire of all the commitments and activities available.

As a coach, I ask people to begin to look at what's truly important to them by slowing down and breathing. Take a few minutes just to notice your breath and clear your head. Then I suggest simply writing in a journal. Start telling the truth to yourself. Ask yourself:

- Is this activity or task enhancing my life or consuming it?
- Does this activity or task reflect who I am and what I value?
- Am I genuinely excited and passionate about what I am doing, or has my life become about *shoulds*?
- Will this activity or task help me get where I want to go?
- If I could live my life any way I wanted, what would it look like?
- Am I staying busy and hectic so I don't have to look at those personal issues that are difficult to address?

Include in your journal an accounting of where you spend your time every day for a week. Include sleeping time, working, commuting, worrying, errands, time for children, quiet time for yourself, etc. You may be very surprised.

When you're immersed in a hectic schedule, it's easy to lose track of how you're spending your time, especially if your priorities are out of order. After looking at how you are spending your time, you can evaluate the list and consciously choose new priorities based on what is really important in your life.

There is a wonderful little story that a colleague shared with me. It goes like this:

An American businessman was at the pier of a small coastal Mexican village when a small boat with just one fisherman docked. Inside the small boat were several large yellow-fin tuna. The American complimented the Mexican on the quality of his fish and asked how long it took to catch them. The Mexican replied, "Only a little while." The American then asked why he didn't stay out longer and catch more fish?

The Mexican said he had enough to support his family's immediate needs. The American then asked, "But what do you do with the rest of your time?"

The fisherman said, "I sleep late, fish a little, play with my children, take siesta with my wife, Maria, stroll into the village each evening where I sip wine and play guitar with my amigos. I have a full and busy life, Señor".

The American scoffed. "I am a Harvard MBA and could help you. You should spend more time fishing, and with the proceeds buy a bigger boat. With the proceeds of the bigger boat you could buy several boats, and eventually you would have a fleet of fishing boats. Instead of selling your catch to a middleman, you could sell directly to the processor, eventually opening your own cannery. You could control the product, the processing and the distribution. You would need to leave this small coastal fishing village and move to Mexico City, then to Los Angeles and eventually to New York City where you will run your own enterprise."

The fisherman asked, "But Señor, how long will this all take?"

To which the businessman replied, "15 to 20 years."

"But what then, Señor?"

The businessman laughed and said, "That's the best part. When the time is right, you would announce an IPO and sell your company stock to the public and become very rich. You would make millions."

"Millions, Señor? Then what?"

The American said, "Then you would retire. Move to a small coastal fishing village where you would sleep late, fish a little, play with your grand-kids, take siesta with your wife, stroll to the village in the evenings, where you could sip wine and play your guitar with your amigos."

Not everything we do, needs to be a goal that is measurable and has an end date. Not everything we accomplish needs to be a *push* or a struggle in order for it to be fulfilling.

If we are willing to relax into life and trust ourselves, we find ourselves being *pulled* toward something important to us, as if we were pulled in the current of a river, rather than trying to push our way upstream.

Plugging the energy drains

We humans tolerate a lot in our lives. We have been brought up with messages like these. Life is tough. Don't rock the boat. Don't complain. Be grateful for what you've got.

At times this may have been good advice, but it can leave us feeling resigned to putting up with all kinds of things that hold us back, cause us grief or waste our time and energy. These are the things I call *tolerations*. When people tolerate, they and their work become mediocre; they get tired. They have to use unhealthy energy sources, such as sugar, caffeine or adrenaline to perform, and natural creativity is squelched. Tolerations are like holes in the water glass of life. No matter how much water you put in, the glass is never full and the water (energy) is constantly drained.

The areas to look in to see what you are tolerating can be: home environment, work environment, career, relationships—or your own bad habits. Make a list of five things you are tolerating at work. Some of them may be: Inadequate training, inadequate workspace, poor communication with someone, inadequate pay, an always-cluttered desk or being overloaded with e-mail and voice mail.

Make a list of ten things you are tolerating at home. Some of them may be: not getting along with your spouse, kids are too (you name it), don't feel good in the geographical location, house needs repairs, too much clutter, car doesn't run well, brown spot on the carpet gets ignored.

Make a list of five things you are tolerating about yourself. Some of them may be: hair is not flattering, nails need a good manicure, haven't been to the dentist in a year, not exercising, eating foods that are not healthy, not getting enough sleep, out of touch with close friends.

You already know that every action you take uses energy. What you may not realize, is that actions you don't take use energy as well—mental energy, emotional energy, energy that could be used in a more productive way. The clutter in your office distracts you and drains your energy. The money problems you've been avoiding keep you awake at night. The items on your mental *to-do* list make you feel guilty and drain the energy you need to accomplish your goals.

After you review the *tolerations* list and are aware of what's draining you, you can begin to focus on handling the things you've been putting off and putting up with. As you start to take action, you will immediately feel energy returning. Start by removing obstacles that prevent you from making an item, such as regular exercise, a priority.

Next look to see which items you can delegate. Perhaps you can involve the family more in daily tasks—or even hire a neighborhood teenager. What errands can get accomplished without you doing them? Look to see what requests you need to make, particularly at work—especially those you have been afraid to make because of perceived adverse consequences. You really don't need to control everything—put yourself in the passenger's seat for awhile.

Let go of unhealthy relationships that you have been stuck in and have been avoiding taking action on. If you know a relationship no longer serves you, your life can change for the better by letting go.

One way to handle the *tolerations* is to use the 3D's—Do it, Delegate it or Dump it.

Do it. Put it on your calendar as a priority and do it now. Schedule the time and, get it done and cross it off your list. No more waiting. You'll get lots of energy from this.

Delegate it. If it isn't the best use of your time, yet you have deemed it important, find someone else who would enjoy doing it. This may be for money, or trade for services. Just get it done. Examples could be laundry, shopping or errands.

Dump it. If something has been hanging around on your calendar or on your mind, and it is not important to you right now, don't do it and don't even think about it. Store the idea somewhere such as your calendar, or a *someday* list, and visit it again in a few months.

Raising your standards and extending your boundaries.

In coaching technology, *standards* are the behaviors or targets of excellence that you hold yourself to; *boundaries* are limits you place on what other people or environments cannot do to you or around you. So boundaries are basically a "no." "No, you cannot ignore me." "No, you may not yell at me." "No, you may not dump that task on me."

Since standards are what *you* do, they are basically a "yes". "Yes, I treat others the way I want to be treated." "Yes, I don't tolerate much." "Yes, I take excellent care of myself." But be careful not to lump your *shoulds* and *coulds* in with your standards. *Shoulds* and *coulds* are behaviors or actions that either you are not ready for yet, or are not right for you. Life is too short for *shoulds* and *coulds*. Don't try to force yourself to raise your standards; rather learn to sense which ones are ready to be naturally raised.

Here is an example of raising a standard. "I always pay my bills." This is a good standard. A raised standard is: "I always pay my bills on time." An even higher one is: "I pay my bills early, before they are due." And a super high standard is: "I don't have bills anymore."

Four step technology to setting a boundary

A boundary is an imaginative circle you draw around yourself, to protect yourself against the negative behaviors of others, not to keep people away from you. Let's say someone you know well is always yelling at you.

1. Inform the person they are stepping over a boundary. You can say "Are you aware you are yelling at me?" Sometimes they don't know. If they don't stop, go to step 2.
2. Ask them to stop. Say, "Please stop yelling now." If they persist, go to step 3.
3. Demand they stop. "Stop that now!" Say it strongly, but without yelling and without threats. It's rare that someone will continue, but if they do, go to step 4.
4. Leave the room. Simply get up and walk out, without slamming doors or other uproar. If the person is in your room, office or space, ask them to leave. It doesn't take very long for someone to figure out you mean business.

Boundaries and standards are like training wheels; they are often helpful when beginning. Becoming aware of boundaries and standards and focusing on extending boundaries and raising standards are key elements in strengthening your quality of life. In coaching terms, I refer to this as the *personal foundation* process. Successfully handling these areas permits people to really be themselves and make the most of life. Boundaries keep us safer from threats, whether real or imagined. Standards give us the opportunity to develop our highest selves, enjoy life and share the gifts we have been given.

Training wheels on bikes can become a limiting factor by both fostering dependency and preventing riders from leaning into the curves as they need to. In the same way, focusing on standards and boundaries becomes less appropriate once we have developed our reserve levels, started attracting instead of chasing and become completely responsible for everything in our lives. I'm not advocating forgetting about our standards and boundaries, I am saying that if we begin to define ourselves by them, we can end up validating ourselves externally. We can become dependent on them, and consequently, not stretch our skills. We will always have our standards and boundaries, and will continue to extend and raise them, but they become less of a focus, or measurement, of our development. We build those muscles and create a self-managing system that requires little attention.

Boundaries and standards will never become automatic if you have major *incompletions* in your life—things left unfinished. If you have issues that you need a therapist to help you work out, if you are addicted to substances, if you are compulsive or have a lot of *tolerations*, then these factors will prevent the natural development of boundaries and standards. Your attempt to develop them under these circumstances will seem forced and unnatural. Boundaries and standards need lots of room to develop themselves, just as a new bike rider needs lots of room to practice. Focusing on the foundation of eliminating *tolerations* and *incompletions* will naturally lead you to want to raise your standards and extend boundaries.

CHAPTER FIVE

INTIMATE RELATIONSHIPS

Rising in love instead of falling in love

Women are the best chameleons. From minute to minute we appear as wives, nurturers, lovers, friends, mothers, politicians, executives, daughters, workers, gardeners, housekeepers, head chefs and chief-cook-and-bottle-washers. Then we change into Superwomen. Whatever is needed, we make sure it gets done. We find ourselves responsible for getting the food, taking the initiative in sex, beautifying our homes and maintaining our children's security. Meanwhile, we stay feminine and strong, speaking our minds without passively giving in or in aggressive arguing.

Exercise: SUPERHUMAN

To what extent do you play the superhuman role? Check each statement that describes you.

- I rarely have a minute to myself.
- I find it very difficult to say no to a worthy cause or person requesting my involvement.
- I frequently try to solve everyone's problems.
- I drag myself to business meeting with the flu rather than delegate the job to someone else.
- I receive a constant string of phone calls all weekend.
- I always do it myself rather than ask for assistance.
- I feel compelled to find ways to make anything I do better than ever before.
- In coaching my child's team, I insist on winning instead of encouraging the kids to learn and enjoy the game.

If you answered yes to more than half, your may be stretching yourself thin among work family, social, professional, and academic responsibilities.

* * *

Sometimes we feel overwhelmed, unsupported and overstressed from our many self-imposed demands. In the face of all this, how can we fulfill our own our emotional needs for lasting intimacy—and passion—in our relationships and in our lives?

This chapter is geared to the midlife woman who wears many hats, who tries to be everything to everyone and who wants more balance while maintaining a quality life. For those who are without a partner and want one, I will discuss appropriate techniques for finding a mate. Along with that discussion, I will deal with building self-esteem, feeling better about oneself, developing better relationships and creating better personal skills for interacting with our families.

The hunt for your soul-mate

The chances of a midlife woman finding a suitable man and marrying him are less than that of being struck by lightening, so dating can become a combat zone instead of a pleasure palace. The key to finding that happy relationship lies in learning to be open to new possibilities. Learn how to bring new people into your life. Focus intently on meeting your intimacy needs socially, emotionally and spiritually. How do are you to go about all this? *What can you realistically expect?*

> *Get out and be seen.*
> *Don't make yourself the world's best kept*
> **SECRET**

Women are now meeting men through personal ads, singles clubs, singles trips, matchmaking services, the internet and even the produce aisle of the local supermarket. My divorced friend planned a vacation with the sole intention of meeting appropriate single men. Her research led her to sign up for a one-week fly-fishing adventure. She was the only woman with 12 single men. As the female star, not only was she catered to for the whole week, but she also made 12 new friends (think of them as options) to keep in touch with. Creativity pays off. Think of whom you want to attract into your life and plan accordingly. If you want athletic friends, go to a health club or join an adventure travel club or a sporting club. If you like literature, go to literary society meetings. There are niches for anyone and everyone, of course.

Let your light shine

To attract, you must signal. How does a woman radiate sexuality and sensuality? I spell it **A-T-T-I-T-U-D-E**. Attitude seems like such a little thing, but it makes a big difference. With an attitudinal change, not only do people see you differently, you perceive and experience differently. *Notice that a 100,000-watt positive charge does you little good if you surround yourself with one million watts of negativity.* To become this new you, you must de-construct your subconscious mind, root out negative attitudes and surround yourself with positive ones.

Repetition powerfully implants new thoughts in your fertile brain. Write down what you do want or who you want to become over and over again. Think about those new ideas as often as you can for the first week. Notice your feelings about what you write and think, and you will soon have that new image conditioned in your outlook.

What we *want* and what we *need* can be two very different things. If you want love, make sure that you look in appropriate places. Too often women I know are confident that their present relationship is different from the other previous ones, yet they keep having the same problems.

The faces may have changed, but having been attracted to a personality similar to that of their former loves, they find themselves in similar conflicts and challenges. If you always act the way you did in the past, why would you expect anything to change? To break the old pattern, you must know what you want and what you need. Then focus on what you need from a relationship and act to attract it. When you are aligned with your best interests, you radiate the inner strength and calmness that attracts exactly the energy you are searching for.

Some women spend years looking for "Mr. Right." Frequently this amounts to turning to others to fill a void of loneliness—and ending up in dependent relationships. Loneliness must be resolved from the inside out—not the other way around. The process involves learning to overcome the fear of aloneness by finding pleasure in being alone with oneself. It is important to note that when you let someone go who is not right, you make room for someone else who is.

Once again, the more we get aligned with our best interests, the more we radiate strength and calmness to attract exactly that energy back to us. Usually, we don't decide to love someone. The feelings either arise or they don't. If feelings of love do arise, we have the alternatives: to accept them or to ignore them. If you have been abused or abandoned by people you cared about in the past, you are likely to play it safe and automatically reject your feelings rather than entrust someone with your affection. Weigh the differences between acceptable risks and missed opportunities for a potentially great relationship.

Passion often brings people together. Learn to sustain your passion for life. Often relationships end when physical passion ends, but learning to accept a new form of passion can keep relationships alive. Passion often changes as we get older, going from physical to emotional and spiritual. You can create more realistic expectations for yourself if you recognize the naturalness of changes in passion for your relationships, your job, your friends and life in general.

Continuing commitment is an integral part of a viable relationship; yet commitment may take many forms as time goes on. "Till death do us part" originated in the Middle Ages when the average life span was 35 years. Now, with life expectancies of over 75 years, commitment may have to be redefined and renegotiated several times over the life of a relationship.

Long-term relationships are in jeopardy unless people learn new skills that bring them face-to-face with the evolving nature of those relationships. Be introspective. Are your feelings being driven by the negative behavior patterns you might have learned while growing up, or are you acting honestly in the present in business, with friends or with your family? If you spend energy on justifying what is wrong, you don't have time or energy left for building on what's right. See others as they are, not as something you can tap for their potential. Ask yourself these questions:

- What does *attaining intimacy* mean to me?
- How are both party's lives more rewarding because of this relationship?
- How can I connect this relationship meaningfully to the personal growth cycle I'm in?

Sometimes there is conflict between what we wish we had and how we go about trying to get it. Many of us have found that, as we tried renegotiating our relationships, we had *deal-breakers* that couldn't be resolved. As a result, many of us have changed spouses or started new households.

Even if you are with the same person for years, your priorities will probably change. There are new challenges and opportunities everywhere you look. You may be chronologically older every day, but as long as you feel young at heart, you have the ability to send out new shoots and grow.

The child within you is that special part that adds sparkling spontaneity, laughter, risk-taking and zest to your life. Sometimes these qualities are buried alive under layers of shame, unresolved grief and anger. Awaken the child within you, and become fully present to the world with renewed excitement. Allow that spark to become an integral part of your existence. When you are childlike in that way, then the world is perceived as a joyful place.

When you are childish, you focus on your own needs and wishes with little or no awareness of or concern for others. For example, it is childish behavior to refuse to turn down the sound on the television or stereo when your mate is trying to concentrate. On the other hand, when you are childlike, you enjoy the benefits of both adult perspective and child responses. You are able to benefit from joy and fun without losing the complex good judgment of adulthood. Childlike fun is never at the expense of someone else. You can retain all the benefits of adult wisdom while rejuvenating yourself with the freedom, joy and passion of a child.

Often we view intimate partners with a distorted look, responding as adults the same way we had responded as children. Breaking through the patterns set up in our early lives is one way to realistically appreciate the emotions of adult life and relieve much stress and guilt. Conflicts are often blown out of proportion by our emotional needs of the moment. Many of these needs are ones that remain unresolved from the past. Are you reenacting childhood events in adult life (the equivalent of throwing a five-year-old temper tantrum at the age of fifty), and completely baffling everyone around you? Learn to ask yourself, "What is really going on here?" Be brave enough to answer honestly.

As midlife women, we are often caught in the web of influence of others—feeling helpless or feeling a loss of self. Good boundaries keep you whole. Boundary issues involve the things you do to maintain your sense of personal self-sufficiency while developing interdependent relationships with others. Sense when you are being misused or abused—mentally, physically or emotionally. Recognize when you are reliving past experiences rather than relating to situations in the present. To maintain personal wholeness—integrity—you must have personal standards, must know what they are, notice when people violate them and be strong enough to stand up for them. If you divorce, you may experience a dramatic lifestyle change. You will learn new skills of being single in what is essentially a coupled world, skills for balancing the time to manage finances, home, work, children, parents and friends while making a new happy life for your self. Many times women are treated like a pariah when they divorce. Even your best friends may no longer invite you to join them. It is as if they think of you as competing with them for their husbands. While divorced men are a social commodity and are invited to all the social gatherings, divorced women seem to be in abundance, and they are not invited as often. Even if a divorced woman is financially independent, she may be faced with major compromises because of her newly single status. She may have to change friends or neighborhoods and join different clubs and interest groups to have any social connections as her expectations and priorities change.

We prioritize even if we are in the same relationship for years. As we change and grow, we continually add new information, so new patterns of thought come into operation. As midlife women, we now know ourselves better, as well as what we want from life and relationships. Fine-tune those wants and needs, and accept only the best.

Exercise: BALANCING RELATIONSHIPS

Ask yourself, among all the people you are giving to, which ones would you also like to receive something back from? Your children, spouse, friends, or work associates? On a separate piece of paper, jot down the names of the people you spend the most time with each week. Then beside each name rate the quality of that relationship. Use a plus sign to indicate that you receive more than you give to that person, a check mark to indicate that you have a fairly balanced give-and-take relationship, or a minus sign to indicate that you are primarily the supporter of that person's needs. For example, if you walk or carpool with a friend twice a week, are the conversations dominated by your friend's problems and concerns or by yours? Is there an equal give and take of topics that are helpful for the both of you?

Next, take steps to bring balance to your list. You might choose to spend less time with some of your friends who are constantly in crisis. Instead look for the few people that add support and fun to your life. Learn to ask for what you want in advance.

* * *

A relationship becomes the best when it is interwoven into four levels: physical, emotional, mental and spiritual. Initially, attraction is usually on the physical and emotional levels as mental and spiritual interactions take more time to develop between people. When the emotions die down, people often become disappointed if they find that they have little in common intellectually and spiritually. It is important to note that growth comes from loving and not from wanting to be loved.

While a good relationship has an element of commitment, it is not a promise of manufactured love. To last, your role in the relationship must be a reflection of what you genuinely feel, not a projection of an impossible fantasy. An ideal mate is a friend whose passion for you increases the more your diversity is experienced.

> *You can't get ahead when you're trying to get even.*

What we focus on becomes our truths. When we focus on the negatives (and criticism) rather than on love (and compliments), we can become angry and bitter. Keeping score in a relationship generates opposition. Opposing teams are formed and partners become competitors rather than teammates.

Sometimes we look for problems where none exist or destroy our happiness because we think we don't deserve it. Sometimes we work to change a partner, then complain that he is not the same person anymore. We say, "I love you, you're perfect. Now change." It is true that, to keep the magic alive, we must constantly create the unexpected and do unfamiliar things, but we also must remember that we are responsible for our own good time. To be a responsible member of a partnership, you must talk with your partner and teach each other how to be happy.

The secret of staying together is growing together. Good relationships support change. Everyone seems to be in favor of progress, yet the very thought of change frightens most of us. We look for security and avoid peeking over new horizons out of fear. *While the mind is soothed by familiarity, the heart yearns for new things.* Communicating with each other about personal growth is essential. Without it, the relationship emotionally shuts down. Feelings are dissipated, and a vacuum takes their place. This can feel like emotional anesthesia.

You never *have* a relationship, you are *in* one. As a dynamic, living thing, your relationship is not a promise of anything more than today. Let it begin with the real fire of what you already feel, not a projection of some distant fantasy. Take the mutual attraction from where it is now, nurture it and watch it grow.

> Live your life as an exclamation, not an explanation.

What I've Learned

- I've learned that, no matter how much I care, some people just don't care back.
- I've learned that, no matter how good a person is, they're going to hurt you every once in a while, and you must forgive them for that.
- I've learned that money is a lousy way of keeping score.
- I've learned that talking can ease emotional pains.
- I've learned that it takes years to build up trust, and only seconds to destroy it.
- I've learned that true friendship continues to grow, even over the longest distance.
- I've learned that you can do something in an instant that will give you a heart ache for life.
- I've learned that it's not what you have in your life, but who you have in your life.
- I've learned that good friends are family members that we are allowed to choose.
- I've learned that we don't have to change friends if we understand that friends change.
- I've learned that the people you care most about in life are taken from you too soon.
- I've learned that you should always leave loved ones with loving words. It may be the last time you see them.
- I've learned that our background and circumstances may have influenced who we are, but we are responsible for ourselves.
- I've learned that you shouldn't compare yourself to the best others can do, but to the best you can do.
- I've learned that it's not where I am that is important. It's where I am going.
- I've learned that, no matter how thin you slice it, there are always two sides.
- I've learned that it takes a long time to become the person I want to be.
- I've learned that it's a lot easier to react than it is to think.

- I've learned that you can keep going long after you think you cannot.
- I've learned that either you control your attitude, or it controls you.
- I've learned that heroes are the people who do what has to be done when it needs to be done, regardless of the consequences.
- I've learned that patience takes a lot of practice.
- I've learned that there are people who love you dearly, but just don't know how to show it.
- I've learned that my best friend and I can do anything or nothing and have the best time.
- I've learned that sometimes the people you expect to kick you when you're down will be the ones to help you get back up.
- I've learned that there is more of my parents in me that I thought.
- I've learned that sometimes when I'm angry I have the right to be angry, but that doesn't give me the right to be cruel.
- I've learned that just because someone doesn't love you the way you want him or her to doesn't mean s/he doesn't love you with all s/he has.
- I've learned that maturity has more to do with what types of experiences you've had and what you've learned from them and less to do with how many birthdays you've celebrated.
- I've learned that you should never tell a child his or her dreams are unlikely or outlandish. Few things are more humiliating, and what a tragedy it would be if s/he believed it.
- I've learned that it isn't always enough to be forgiven by someone else. Sometimes you have to learn to forgive yourself.
- I've learned that, no matter how bad your heart is broken, the world doesn't stop for your grief.

The Difference Between Men and Women

Here is a story that might help you understand how men and women think differently about relationships. Let's say a man named Roger is attracted to a woman named Elaine. He asks her out to a movie; she accepts; they have a pretty good time. A few nights later he asks her out to dinner, and again they enjoy themselves.

They continue to see each other regularly, and after a while neither one of them is seeing anybody else. And then, one evening when they're driving home, a thought occurs to Elaine, and, without really thinking, she says it aloud. "Do you realize that, as of tonight, we've been seeing each other for exactly six months?" And then there is silence in the car. To Elaine, it seems like a very loud silence.

She thinks to herself *I wonder if it bothers him that I said that. Maybe he's been feeling confined by our relationship; maybe he thinks I'm trying to push him into some kind of obligation that he doesn't want, or isn't sure of.*

And Roger is thinking *Gosh. Six months.*

And Elaine is thinking *But, hey, I'm not so sure I want this kind of relationship, either. Sometimes I wish I had a little more space so I'd have time to think about whether I want us to keep going the way we are, moving steadily forward. I mean, where are we going? Are we just going to keep seeing each other at this level of intimacy? Are we heading toward marriage? Toward children? Toward a lifetime together? Am I ready for that level of commitment? Do I really even know this person?*

And Roger is thinking *So that means it was—let's see—February when we started going out, which was right after I had the car at the dealer's, which means...lemme check the odometer.... Whoa! I am way overdue for an oil change here.*

And Elaine is thinking *He's upset. I can see it on his face. Maybe I'm reading this completely wrong. Maybe he wants more from our relationship, more intimacy, more commitment; maybe he has sensed—even before I sensed it—that I was feeling some reservations. Yes, I bet that's it. That's why he's so reluctant to* say anything about his own feelings. He's afraid of being rejected.

And Roger is thinking *And I'm gonna have them look at the transmission again. I don't care what they say, it's still not shifting right. And they better not try to blame it on the cold weather this time. I paid them 600 dollars.*

And Elaine is thinking *He's angry. And I don't blame him. I'd be angry too. I feel so guilty, putting him through this, but I can't help the way I feel. I'm just not sure.*

And Roger is thinking *They'll probably say it's only a 90-day warranty.*

And Elaine is thinking *I'm just too idealistic, waiting for a knight to come riding up on his white horse, when I'm sitting right next to a perfectly good person, a person I enjoy being with, a person I truly do care about, a person who seems to truly care about me, a person who is in pain because of my self-centered, schoolgirl romantic fantasy.*

And Roger is thinking *Warranty? They want a warranty? I'll tell them what they can do with the warranty.*

"Roger," Elaine says aloud.

"What?" says Roger, startled.

"Please don't torture yourself like this," she says, her eyes beginning to brim with tears. "Maybe I should never have ... Oh, I feel so..." She breaks down, sobbing.

"What?" says Roger.

"I'm such a fool," Elaine sobs. "I mean, I know there's no knight. I really know that. It's silly There's no knight, and there's no horse?"

"There's no horse?" says Roger.

"Your think I'm a fool, don't you?" Elaine says.

"No!" says Roger, glad to finally know the correct answer.

"It's just that... It's that I ... I need some time," says Elaine.

There is a 15-second pause while Roger, thinking as fast as he can, tries to come up with a safe response. Finally he comes up with one that he thinks might work.

"Yes," he says.

Elaine, deeply moved, touches his hand. "Oh, Roger, do you really feel that way?" she says.
"What way?" says Roger.
"That way about time," says Elaine.
"Oh," says Roger "Yes."
Elaine turns to face him and gazes deeply into his eyes, causing him to become very nervous about what she might say next, especially if it involves a horse. At last she speaks.
"Thank you, Roger," she says.
"Thank *you*," says Roger.
After he takes her home, she lies on her bed—a conflicted, tortured soul—and weeps until dawn. When Roger gets back to his place, he opens a bag of Doritos, turns on the TV and immediately becomes deeply involved in a rerun of a tennis match between two Czechoslovakians he's never heard of. A tiny voice in the far recesses of his mind tells him that something major was going on back there in the car, but he is pretty sure there is no way he would ever understand what, so he figures it is better if he doesn't think about it.
The next day Elaine will call her closest friend—or perhaps two of them—and they will talk about this situation for six straight hours. In painstaking detail, they will analyze everything she said and everything he said, going over it time and time again, exploring every word, expression, and gesture for nuances of meaning, considering every possible ramification. They will continue to discuss this subject, off and on, for weeks, maybe months, never reaching any definite conclusions, but never getting bored with it, either.
Meanwhile, Roger, while playing racquetball one day with a mutual friend of his and Elaine's, will pause just before serving, frown, and say, "Norm, did Elaine ever own a horse?"

* * *

Relationships: Some Personal Stories

Just as with Roger and Elaine in the previous section, communication between women and men often goes awry. Here are just a few stories that run the gamut of the good times, the in-between times and the I-don't-need-this times. How you handle such situations can transform your thoughts, feelings and actions into positive ones rather than leaving you living dangerously or wallowing in pity. Even if you decide that a life-phase is finished and you want to move on, do it with strength and confidence.

I have been having an affair with a married man for three years now. We are in love and have a great time when we see each other. My friends keep telling me to get out of this affair. I feel it is the actual marriage that I should get out of. There must obviously be a lot wrong with my marriage if I have been searching elsewhere. It has been difficult for me to be living a life of deception and lies. I am willing to get a divorce, but my boyfriend is not. I have some major soul searching to do, or I will be *the other woman* forever.

* * *

I am no longer in love with my husband. We have grown emotionally and spiritually apart and no longer support each other in any aspect of our lives. We constantly repeat the same mistakes. My therapist told me that I will be dissatisfied with any new relationship until I start to take care of myself, know what I do want and go about getting it in a healthy way. She said it is possible to rekindle the romance in my marriage and that it can even be better than before. Our children take up so much of our time that there is no time for each other, so we have drifted apart. My therapist claims that this has become a convenient excuse to not deal with each other—so we can go our own ways and live separate lives under the same roof. Maybe it is time to see if there is any spark left or if all the flames are out.

* * *

I have been a good wife and mother. My children are loved and well-adjusted. My husband is wonderful. Yet with all this greatness, I am contemplating an affair. I want to feel the attention of another man. I have been married for 30 years, and want to feel that lust again. I feel that I am missing exciting romantic adventures, and that episodes with a faceless stranger might satisfy that need. My friends tell me to count my blessings. They say that, if it is erotic sex and lust that I want, I should initiate it—and that my husband can fulfill these fantasies. I don't want to jeopardize our marriage. I just want a temporary change. It may not be worth the consequences.

* * *

I am so comfortable with him, yet there is no passion and lust anymore. I don't even remember what that felt like. I watch romantic movies and cry. I have a strong friendship, but no physical attraction to him anymore. I don't want an affair, yet temptation keeps haunting me. Help!

* * *

I am 60 years of age and have been in love and married to the same wonderful, caring person for 40 years. We have had our ups and downs, but *respect* has kept us together. We each have our own interests and support each other much of the time. We have changed, yet we remain flexible in our changing. As long as this man thinks I am his goddess, he will remain my adored mate. He makes it easy to love him, and I guess I do the same for him.

* * *

I am 46 with three children, ages 13, 8 and 16 months. I am not certain that my toddler is the last. My husband really wants another, which is fine with me too, if it weren't for the genetic risks of my age. What surprised me during my pregnancy with my youngest child was the negative comments from other women about my being pregnant and having a child at my age. There were numerous statements such as, "Thank goodness it is you and not me." One woman said, "If that happened to me, I'd jump of a bridge!" and another added, "I'd be right behind you." I was shocked, hurt and surprised. My other two children are still young, so a new baby is not a major lifestyle change for me, but I believe my children keep me young and vital in thought and in action. Sometimes you just have to do what feels right, and this is right for me.

ADVANCED RELATIONSHIPS

Carlos Warter, M.D.

This chapter speaks about understanding, attaining and improving relationships throughout our lives. The following article by Carlos Warter depicts the ultimate relationship as it intertwines the four levels of the physical, emotional, mental and spiritual. It is truly the advanced course in relationships.

Carlos Warter M.D. Ph.D. is a trained medical doctor with Harvard post-graduate education, transpersonal psychotherapist, and acclaimed author of "Recovery of the Sacred" and "Who Do You Think You Are?; The Healing Power of Your Sacred Self" Born in Chile, he has been awarded the United Nations Peace Messenger and the Pax Mundi awards for his humanitarian efforts. He presents keynote speeches, workshops and seminars throughout the world. Dr. Warter can be reached at his web site www.carloswarter.com, *via e-mail at* cwartermd@aol.com *or by phone at 888-SOULNET.*

You are a sacred being whose true identity is essential. To begin this section, I select a phrase we have heard many times, "Know thyself." But first, let me modify it to "Know thyself as a human being." But what kind of human being? We live overwhelmed by endless thoughts, opinions, discussions, feelings or experiences which we have acquired as a result of our interactions with the environment in which we live. We think that to *know oneself* is simply knowing what we think and what we feel. Yet, behind almost every one of our thoughts and feelings, there is a foreign opinion—the fruit of our education and training—and we seldom ask who or what was it that influenced us to think or feel in this specific way.

If we truly introspect and try to reach the depth of our being, we will find ourselves in a zone of internal silence. And in this silence there is a force, a sensation, which is not merely a physical sensation, but a fullness that says *I am*—not in words but simply in being. When I think then of the phrase "Know thyself" I think of going deep into the core of my being until I reach that point of total abundance. When the inner silence is total, even for an instant, we will feel that all our daily thoughts and all our vital experiences are anecdotal, they have no weight before the fullness of the *I am*. There are thoughts floating around, there are also feelings but we are an impartial observer, a witness to it all.

In this moment something arises, like an inner smile. A certainty arises that all that has happened and is happening is subject to change but we, the witness, are not subject to change. That is why this moment is associated with an experience of light, such that, if one closes one's eyes, the whole body is in silence and enveloped in brightness, as though we were looking with our eyes fixed at the sun with eyelids closed. And what do we feel? There are two basic things that have to do with the development of this sensation of the immanent now. One is the Unifying Consciousness and the other is the Vital Purpose.

The Unifying Consciousness is particular or singular in each individual. This is the *I am*. When an individual enters this space, her essence is accompanied by a greater presence. It is the presence of the Creator. It is the sublime presence of knowing in Divine Aloneness in Pure Presence. This is the common-union, the communion, the domain of knowledge of the loving relationship with the social community. This experience gives us the certainty that each of us is unique. When looking at another person afterwards, we see someone who, at their center, is also unique in a way that transcends all their underlying illusions, thoughts and feelings. This is the creation, to my understanding, of the first order of change in focus. From the *I am*, I address others with respect that implies the recognition that the other is essentially unique as well. In other words, as one becomes conscious of one's own singularity, there is access to the singularity of others.

As for the Vital Purpose—the purpose of life—it is the expression of that singularity, of that diamond, of that unique gem which everyone has. It is different in each, but similar in expression. During all daily contingencies, we can act with or without knowledge of our essence. If we have experienced the introspection that allows us to know ourselves—our vital expression of who we are—each one of our actions, sensations, thoughts and feelings are directed toward one purpose: the manifestation of ourselves and the vision of the essence of all those around us. It is a chain reaction, a true expansion.

There are three phases in this process.

1. Being conscious of what rules us internally, externally, socially and psychically.
2. Transforming our ability to experience life so that we are not ruled by the ordeal of each situation but that we acquire certain mastery over such situations. By this, I do not refer to control or manipulation, but to the grace of peace with certainty and confidence—that the process of life, ever autonomous, flows through these circumstances. Understanding this creates sufficient calmness to project peacefulness in all our actions.
3. Understanding that the existence of the physical being is not the figural occurrence in life. Interpersonal transcendence—going beyond the physical nature of the *I am*—is that which leads to happiness. I call happiness the age of faith, that is, the moment from which faith in our vital core is not only rising above the conditioning of circumstances, but transcends them. At this moment when we know ourselves, we can love truly.

The word love comes from the Etruscan, meaning "remembering ones own divinity"—in other words, sensing the presence of the Creator in us, in our essence. The ancient Greeks had different words for each of the meanings of love. Love between members of the family was fraternal love, *agape* was the name for friendship, and *eros* was sensual love. We have condensed these meanings in the word *love*, in spite of the different qualities of meaning.

The remembrance of our own essence, our divinity, corresponds to essential love—being present in human interactions, with our own consciousness projected towards others. Let us look at an example.

Let us say I see a woman, and a feeling comes up which is neither an emotion nor a fondness but something more profound than emotion and affection. Let us say that I see this woman, and curiously I see her eyes. If I find in her a certain ray of light that is not intimidating—something that signals a person who knows profoundly who she is, who is not identified just with her beautiful body or hairdo or her external appearance—then something happens in me. A certain resonance is evoked in me. I want to get closer to know her more fully and for her to know me. I see details—worldly, physical, circumstantial, emotional details—and I project energy in action, as emotion, into affection itself. Here is where I want to go with this example: learning to love means learning to recognize the divinity in oneself and in the other. The expression of this love is energy in action.

Many times we misunderstand; we believe that what is basic in love is the physical or emotional attraction, even though we know that this quickly passes, that it is born and fades with an effervescence that is surprising. On the other hand, if there is an essential relatedness, it could be that the activities between these people change, that at the beginning there is romance and then a friendship or vice versa. It could be that the passion could be converted to something more calming, more intimate. But the connection will be there forever because that recognition transcends all exterior circumstances.

How many couples do you know who have separated because one of them observes, "Well, he is (or she) is not the same any more"? It is understandable that both have changed physically. Pascal says, "It is natural for a person to say, 'I love you,' now and a moment later say, 'I no longer love you,' because he is no longer the same." It is true that the person now is older, thinner, heavier, etc., but this does not mean that he is not same as he was before.

Due to this ignorance, the love that yesterday united them is veiled from them.

Typically, conventional emotional relationships are based on deficits. What I do not have I substitute with what you have, and what you do not have, I substitute with what I have. This attitude demonstrates the ignorance of the wholeness of each of the lovers, since neither of them bring the fullness of their being, their divine bounty, to the relationship. Consequently, they do not see their own unique and blissfully full singularity. By combining their perceived lack, they condemn their love to extinction sooner or later. If, instead of forging a relationship based on lack, they would have united in fullness, then they would have been free of the anxiety producing process of making one total being by adding between two incomplete ones. When speaking about their couple-counterpart, many people say, "This is my better half." In truth, real interaction occurs when I am a whole and my lover is another whole. Only then do we complement each other in a cornucopia of fullness.

The phrase "Know thyself" raises the diversity of roles that are played out in daily life. The first is essential, or vital, identity. It is simply the *I am* without contingencies. We are our essence in the context of a greater presence. The presence of the creative force (call it God or the unknown or the universe or life itself) is indisputable. Our essence is not manifested in isolation but it appears under the sanctuary of life itself, guarded by the vital force—the breath of divinity—that nurtures it. How do we recognize this vital force? This presence knows how to make itself felt. We recognize it because it is an imposing presence, but, while it surprises, it does not crush. Instead, it nourishes.

Any action has three elements—its purpose, the action itself and the way of doing it. If we do not have consciousness of our vital identity and our *I am*, the vision we will have of ourselves is connected with only the action of what we do. Let us suppose that someone has identified with work. Each time that person looks at her action in the world, she is seeing nothing more than the reflection of her role in the eyes of others. Not only does she act in response to this reflection, but she also proceeds to analyze it, believing it is real. This fantasy only serves to separate her from herself. If we loose connection with our vital identity, and believe that we are only the role—lawyer, mother, citizen, wife, etc.—we will loose the notion of what is true, and we will only be concerned with defending that role at all costs.

The will of the true identity is to protect the being and its intended purpose. By forgetting the being, and adopting the role, instead of gaining genuine protection, we work to insure the survival of a transient belief of the moment.

Contrary to identifying ourselves with what we do, we are called—as our purpose—to love ourselves and to love others. To be truly in love with those I love, I must first be in love with me. Playing the role of couple can confound this. As seen from the outside, the couple acts to be together without taking into account their vital identities. From the inside, however, the commitment is to manifest the *I am* in each lover—my abundance in service to your abundance—that is, I act in the service of total love. This discovery of this wonder becomes the total vindication of essence and vital consciousness. Some would say, "But that would take away our autonomy." This is not true, however, if one chooses to serve from the *I am*. Pure love does not take away anything because it is a communion—a giving together of abundance—between him and her.

We all have the continuous opportunity to contribute in the world; in fact, we are always contributing something to it in spite of our intention. If we look at ourselves biologically, we are machines of absorption and reduction. We take in nutritious things, we absorb what is good for us and we eliminate the remainder. In the field of work, then, there are two fundamental positions from which to consider action. One is the position of abundance. I am here, and I am to serve, not only with my body and my physical work but also with all my being. I have to determine the needs in the environment that I can respond to with the abilities and skills I possess. The other position is that of scarcity. What do I need to do in the world to survive? That notion of *survival* can be further fragmented into financial survival—the way in which I am paid so that I might continue to feed the machine of absorption and reduction that is my body—and affective survival—the way in which I am appreciated, loved or respected so that I can think well of myself. This scarcity-survival position can be simplified as *I am my salary* and *I am what others think of me*. Who can feel free living life like this? The more money a person makes, and the more positive regard that person harvests as a result, the more he or she becomes a slave of others.

What is the difference between external freedom and inner freedom? Internal freedom is the confidence that there is no person who or thing that can modify or distort my essential identity. It is the Creator and the consciousness of our own selves that determines our existence. Realizing this, we accept being fully who we are. Forgetting this, we become distracted from our vital identity and focus our attention externally. We then identify with exterior phenomena and images that we project towards others. As we identify with these external circumstances, there is a sensation of contraction and a loss of freedom that we tend to attribute to the circumstances themselves—because we are unable to look inwardly.

A person who is absolutely "in love" is truly free. She feels a great affinity with the external reality. What greater freedom than to be able to look at the world from the abundance of love?

If we delegate our identification to the circumstances, we say I am free *because* I am in love with him or *because* the day is beautiful or *because* I received a raise in salary or *because* I had certain success. Even though it seems as if this is internal freedom, it is not, because the *I am* is not in the moment. It is as if the *I am* depends for its meaning on external success. The source of internal freedom is transferred to external psychological or social phenomena.

When a society forgets internal freedom and delegates everything to materialism, individuals in that society experience great pressure. This pressure is manifested externally through oppression and repression and internally through mental depression.

It would seem—and I want to make clear that I am talking about appearances and not something that has been proven to be actually occurring—that at the end of the twentieth century, with the our vastly expanded technology, we are like children with too many new toys. We forget ourselves because we are up to our necks in a toy store of objects that keep us hypnotically attracted. We have seen the appearance of many new and strange points of view that are not very deep, but that attract us and trap us. Because of my faith in the evolution of the consciousness of humankind, I think that soon the moment will be here for maturation. We will soon see all technology being used in the service of leisure. We will come to the rediscovery of ourselves and arrive at a better interaction among and use of human resources. I have dedicated my life to this, working for the awakening of the all those who, little by little, are becoming aware that the recovery of the sacred is possible.

All that we really are looking for is love, but the forces that teach us—our parents and society—do not always know how to help us find it. We set out to do things to win their love. As we do this, we interpret any kind of attention as love. We learn that to get that feeling of love from our parents, we have to act and be a certain way. We go through life trained to please others—or perhaps the exact opposite, to be a rebel. In either case, we are allowing ourselves to be manipulated by others. We aren't our true selves.

The first step is to overcome whatever is connecting one's present problems to the negative programming acquired in childhood. To do that, a person must clear this "inherited way of being" or programming and recognize that she is not living her true nature and that she is reacting to others rather than living her own way of being.

Once this clearing is completed, she can gain a maturity of the heart and grow to be responsible for her own actions and essence.

Forgiveness of past wrongs and a deepened compassion for others are key outcomes that facilitate inner healing. People who reach this stage gain happiness, confidence and self-satisfaction because they are living in alignment with themselves. This allows for the free flow of feelings, thoughts, and intuition that keeps us growing and developing.

> *With some relationships you spend a lifetime; with others you invest it. Invest wisely!*

CHAPTER SIX

MIDLIFE IN THE WORKPLACE

Many women want to reenter the workforce and find that their credentials are no longer valid, the career landscape has changed, and they are not qualified to make a decent living. Most women didn't have masculine role models for work. We generally played with dolls and stuffed animals and learned to be the nurturers and caregivers. As a result, it is often difficult for us to maintain feminine traits such as compassion in decision making in the workplace. As women, we had always learned to temper judgment with compassion—that not everything is a bottom line decision. We navigate life with cooperation not competition, and we think in terms of abundance not scarcity. Women have learned how to fulfill their needs first so they would not be depleted and then give what is necessary to others.

> Be pro-active.
> Don't let life happen to you.
> Make life happen for you.

We are successful because of our ability to use strong networking support groups and our good communication skills. We are also noted for our ability to negotiate, to accommodate and to cooperate. When we are emotionally secure, we feel safe to take risks in the business world.

Even so, the going can be tough. There are still companies that will not take an attractive woman seriously. As a bright, effective boss with male peers and subordinates, a woman might face many challenges that would not occur for a man. In addition, women often must leave their home as a caring mom, go to work in a competitive rather than cooperative atmosphere, and then revert to that nurturing personality before reaching home again. These are just some of the many adjustments a courageous working woman must make. Besides being paid, most of us also need to feel appreciated, trusted, worthy, sensitive and validated. Those kinds of rewards are not typically what the business world is prepared to deliver.

> *It is more important HOW we accomplish than WHAT we accomplish.*

As a result of more women rising in the public life of commerce, education and government, we have the power to modify how the world looks at itself and how it rewards the players in the game of life. Nowhere is that power more evident than in the lives of working midlife women. For us, work is love made visible. At this time in our lives, we are less concerned about what we receive and more concerned about what we become. We have the power to change the world.

Every one of us changes history and creates the future by the actions we take, whomever we may touch or whatever we may affect. Everything we do changes a situation, and therefore, the world. Rather than dwelling on how far we are from perfection, be immersed in every experience. Mistakes are never losses if we learn from them and move on.

> *What lies behind us and what lies before us are tiny matters compared to what lies within us.*
> *— Oliver Wendell Holmes*

Exercise: ACCENTUATE THE POSITIVE

The easiest way to actually see what you consider your strengths and where you need to improve is to draw three columns on a piece of paper. Label the first column STRENGTHS and list all of yours in this section. Label the second column IMPROVEMENTS; under this heading, note where you need to improve. This could be what you don't feel you do well or just don't like to do even though you have to. Label the third column CHANGE; under this heading, list steps you can take to move the items in column two into column one.

You don't have to reinvent the wheel to transmute your less effective efforts into positive ones. For instance, if you like to travel yet you don't like to spend time in the car, your method of coping better could be listening to audiotapes of music, stories or lectures so that the time passes quickly. As another example, you may love your job, but dislike your office space. Transforming it with pictures, flowers or your own personal touch could change this environment into someplace pleasurable. A third example could be that you know that exercise is good for you, but you don't like to do it. The method for change may be to incorporate it into your regular routine—stretches while ironing; squats while putting things away; or lunges while vacuuming or sweeping. Go to a personal trainer to learn the correct way of doing these motions; that way you will get the most benefit from them and not get hurt from improper movements. A creative idea can make the most unpleasant task pleasurable.

* * *

A midlife woman can make powerfully appropriate decisions because her mind is balanced and clear. With renewed confidence you can live life with that kind of passion and energy. Create a life that surmounts any challenges as you travel a road of discovery and adventure. Generate new circumstances for yourself to renew passion.

Responding to the new will keep you young and enable you to cultivate the wisdom that is dormant within you. When your seeds of experience, awareness and imagination take root, you have the capacity to expand and grow in your own Garden of Eden.

> *Choice is always there for you.*

THE PATH OF SUCCESS

The dictionary defines success as a favorable result. Most people describe happiness as the ultimate wished-for ending. Happiness, however, is not a goal. It is an ongoing process of daily choices and decisions. Success and winning are not measured by what you have. You can be rich and happy or rich and miserable. Winning is assessed by how you feel about life, which is determined by what your life is about. A career is goal oriented, but a vocation, or calling, focuses on the purpose of your life. Your vocation should guide and influence your choices of career.

What is Life?

These guides can create a new way of looking at life and present a target for success that is beyond fame or fortune—a peaceful soul.

> Life is a gift—accept it
> Life is an adventure—risk it
> Life is a mystery—unfold it
> Life is a game—play it
> Life is struggle—face it
> Life is beauty—praise it
> Life is a puzzle—solve it
> Life is opportunity—take it
> Life is sorrowful—experience it

> Life is a song—sing it
> Life is a goal—achieve it
> Life is a mission—accomplish it

As Robert Kennedy said, "Few will have the greatness to bend history itself, but each of us can work to change a small portion of events... It is from numberless acts of courage and belief that human history is shaped." History is created both by the celebrated and by the unknown.

Here is an example. There were thousands of starfish washed up on the shore. A boy was picking them up one by one and throwing them back into the ocean. A passer by asked the boy how saving a few would make any difference. The boy picked up a starfish and, as he threw it back into the water, said, "It's going to make a lot of difference to this one."

It's important to somehow make a contribution to the world. Understand that you bring something special that no one else can offer. It is said that we were born to be thoroughly used up by the time we die. The meaning of this is that we were created to fulfill a purpose that empowers, inspires and gives meaning to our lives—and fulfilling that purpose will take all our energy.

Many feel that the purpose of life is to make a profit. Keeping in the terminology of business, the purpose of life really is to find, satisfy and keep a customer. Opportunities to do this occur when there is a problem to be solved or a need to be met. Profit then becomes the result and reward of doing the right things and doing things right. The customer may be humanity, the world or the universe. Who knows?

To keep you focused on things like monetary profit, the essence of who you are has been covered up over the years by layers of beliefs and assumptions about yourself and others. Many of these conclusions are based on erroneous information. They seem true to you only because you believe them to be. Conditional love, for example, is not love at all but merely approval for meeting someone else's standards.

The heart's memory eliminates the bad and magnifies the good, however, and thanks to this artifice, we manage to endure the erroneous. As Henny Youngman said, "If you're going to do something tonight that you'll be sorry for tomorrow morning, sleep late." Isn't it time to wake up?

Releasing Negative Thoughts Sets You Free

What frame of mind would you like to be in at the beginning of each day? What feelings would you like to experience at the end of the day? After you are gone, what would you like people to say about you? What do you want your life to stand for; to represent?

Determine what you represent and fill in the four columns below—my assets-my skills-my talents-my strengths—as a first step toward achieving some new goals. How would you like to be remembered? What have you always dreamed of contributing to the world? Looking back on your life, what are some of your major contributions? When people think of you, what might they say are your most outstanding characteristics?

	My Assets	My Skills	My Talents	My Strengths
I would like to be remembered for…				
What attributes I would use to make a major contribution to the world…				
Some of my major achievements come from…				
People would say my most outstanding characteristics are…				

What Do You Really Want From Your Life's Work?

Complete the statements below as a way to describe your purpose and character to various audiences, first to an intimate friend, second to your family and third to your coworkers and fourth as an introduction to people who do not know you yet. Think about it first, then write your four statements.

1 (To my closest friend) I am...
2. (To my family) I am...
3. To my coworkers) I am...
4. (To strangers who I want to know me) I am...

How close are the four descriptions to each other? Are you a different person to different people? Is this because you are trying to be what they want you to be? When you are being the best *you* possible, you will want to look the same to everyone.

Know what vision of yourself you want. To make that vision a reality, begin by ignoring the *how* and concentrating on the *what*. Just believe that somehow the transformation is possible, then you can accomplish it.

Here are some common barriers that keep people from trusting they can get what they want.

1. Lack of awareness that we have considerable influence over the outcomes of our lives. (Successful people are not just lucky but have planned, designed, and worked hard for their place in the world.)
2. The feeling of being undeserving of achieving our dreams.
3. Cultural conditioning that limits how we define or measure success. (Will Rogers said, "Half our life is spent trying to find something to do with the time we have rushed through life trying to save.")

Create a new vision by laying out everything you are today and daring to imagine a new life. Let your imagination run free. Think about all those desires, dreams, hopes and fantasies (anything you have wanted to do or be that focuses on nourishing your spirit). Now put these visions into four categories. Personal, Family, Career and Spiritual. Think like a person of action, then act like a person of thought. Turn your visions into goals. Treat those goals as guides. They should stretch and challenge you but not defeat you. You have is no guarantee of ever reaching a goal or reaching it at a certain time, but there is an absolute guarantee of never attaining goals that are never set and never acted on.

A positive attitude sees a problem as an opportunity, a difficulty as a challenge. Take on the attitude that you will not be defeated, no matter what challenges life presents. The positive thinker regards life as an adventure where the rewards are in the risks and the pleasures are in responding to the challenges.

A happy person is not a person in a certain set of circumstances, but rather a person with a certain set of attitudes. Whether life is a privilege or a pain has nothing to do with the circumstances of our lives. It is a direct reflection of our attitudes. A positive attitude is a choice. It is said that the more problems you have, the more alive you are.

You must also have commitment. No matter how noble your purpose, how clear your vision, how explicit your goals or how positive your attitude, what you have envisioned for your future will remain a dream unless you are willing to take a committed stand. There is a difference between involvement and commitment. When you are involved in doing something, you can come and go. When you are committed to something, it means your life. (It is said that, when it comes to bacon and eggs, the hen is involved, but the pig is committed.)

The key element common to many successful people is not talent but an extraordinary drive and determination. Anna Pavlova said, "No one can arrive [at success] from being talented alone. God gives talent; work transforms talent into genius." Of course, only you can determine whether the rewards you look forward to are worth the effort.

Commitment is the mental resolve never to give up. Keeping a commitment or a promise delivers a major deposit into your Emotional Bank Account, breaking a promise is a major withdrawal. Take notice if you are well funded or overdrawn in your account-ability.

Determined action is the evidence of the resolve of commitment, and success requires both mental and physical effort. The alternative—the life of the uncommitted person—means no compelling reason to get up in the morning. One day follows another with the only goal being survival. Vacillating on the smallest of decisions and making mountains of molehills are the ways the uncommitted alleviate boredom.

Growing and contributing are the great purposes on the path of life. The committed person follows this path with openness and flexibility. As a result, a committed person encounters synchronicity. Synchronicity is the attraction of circumstances into our lives that support the accomplishment of what we desire. Jonathan Winters said, "I couldn't wait for success, so I went ahead without it." As you venture bravely on the path, consider also Jonathan Swift's wish, "May you live all the days of your life." and Ernest Becker's observation, "What we fear is not so much extinction, but extinction with insignificance." On his 94th birthday, George Burns was asked if he felt he would live to be 100. He answered, "I have to, I'm booked." Jack Nicklaus put it this way, "Maybe I'll win, maybe I won't play well and won't win. But whatever happens, I'll learn something from it."

With imagination, courage and commitment, people like you have transcended to new levels of personal fulfillment. Isn't it your turn?

FIVE BARRIERS TO ASKING FOR WHAT YOU WANT

- *Ignorance*—Don't realize you can ask.
- *Erroneous Beliefs*—Don't really know what you want.
- *Fear*—Afraid of receiving a negative answer and being humiliated.
- *Pride*—Resentful resistance to revealing needs or wants.
- *Low Self-Esteem*—Not feeling worthy of asking for and receiving help.

Ignorance

Here is a story. A seamstress creates a gorgeous gown adorned with intricate beadwork and sells it through her normal connections. A friend asks her how much she sold it for, and she replies, "Fifty dollars." The friend expresses amazement that the reward was so small. The seamstress replies, "You mean there is a higher number?"

Many of us don't know what we are worth or what to ask for. Others of us are not able to perceive our real needs and wants. We haven't learned how to make an effective request, whom or when to ask nor how to interpret the non-verbal cues that people send. It always seems to be other people who are buying a house with no money down, requesting a lower interest rate on their credit cards, getting a free upgrade on their car rental or negotiating a less expensive rate on their hotel room,

It could be that we are not in touch with our real needs and desires now because we were ignored, rejected or shamed for expressing our thoughts, or criticized, ridiculed, resented, threatened or punished for voicing our wants in the past. If that happened frequently, we probably denied feeling what we wanted because it was too painful. Typically, we never received any modeling or mentoring in clear asking, making effective requests or communicating effectively.

Limiting Beliefs

For most of us, negative beliefs have been programmed into our subconscious and now control much of our behaviors. Born with an empty data bank, we have been programmed by parents, teachers, peers and the media. We have been taught:

- It is better to give than to receive.
- If he really loved me, I wouldn't have to ask.
- Being needy is weak.
- If you don't ask for much, you won't be disappointed.
- It is safer to keep quiet and look smart than speak and be held to be a fool.

Taught to be gentle, we were not expected to make requests. We were not asked our preferences and were not given choices. We were told where to go, what to eat, and when to speak. (At the same time, men were learning to be forceful, and that real men never expressed deep needs or vulnerability.) We were taught that there is never enough time, enough food, enough money or enough attention to go around. We learned to suffer through a boring job as it is better than nothing.

Fear

Fears of rejection, appearing dumb, powerlessness, humiliation, punishment, abandonment or obligation can freeze us before we ask. Only our own mind can produce fear, however.

Pride

We are convinced that we need to do everything ourselves or we risk a loss of self respect and violate our own sense of adequacy.

Low self-esteem

According to studies, only one of every three people has high self-esteem. Most of us feel unworthy in the pursuit of love and happiness, suffer from guilt and lack self-confidence. As a result, we believe our needs and wants are unimportant and unworthy. We are prone to co-dependency since we believe that other people's needs are more important than our own.

> *Change your won't power to will power*
>
> - *If you don't ask, you don't get*
> - *"It's a funny thing about life; if you refuse to accept anything but the best, you very often get it."*
>   — Somerset Maugham

Seven characteristics of people who receive what they want

1. They know what they want. They are clear about their purpose, their vision and their goals.
2. They believe they are worthy of receiving it.
3. They believe they can get it
4. They are passionate about it.
5. They take action in the face of fear.
6. They learn from their experience.
7. They are persistent.

> *The only way to discover the limits of the possible is to go beyond — then into the impossible.*

To know what you want, make a list of 101 wishes. Be specific. Once you commit to having something, your mind will figure out how to get it. What do you desire in these areas?

- Marriage and love relationships
- Family and friends
- Home; cars; clothes
- Job and career
- Money and finances

- Achievements
- Health
- Recreation and free time
- Personal growth
- Things you would like to contribute to your community

Once you know what you want, you must deepen the passion by believing it is possible to get it. Visualize the result as if it had already been accomplished. This builds up a mental force that motivates you and propels you into action.

> *Success isn't a result of spontaneous combustion. You must set yourself on fire.*

Five Steps to Conquer Fear

1. Realize that you create your fears.
2. Analyze your fears. What's the worst thing that could happen? What is the best thing? What is the real likelihood of each?
3. Use positive self-talk.
4. Experience fear so you learn to carry on even if you are afraid. Growth and development require some discomfort. Life is a series of new experiences. Those experiences can be viewed as unwanted pains or as adventures of potential.
5. Reframe the meaning of rejection.

Learning how to ask

- Ask as if you expect to get it.
- Ask someone who can give it to you.
- Make sure you have the other person's full attention.
- Be clear and specific. If you are clear about what you want, your brain will figure out how to make it happen.
- Ask for what you do want, not the absence or cessation of what you *don't* want.
- Ask with *passion*. Eye contact is very important.

- Humor and creativity impresses. Remember, you have to give to get. Give compliments or praise. State how your request benefits the other person.

Words of Wisdom

- Life is the greatest bargain; we get it for nothing.
- The secret of staying young is to live honestly, eat slowly and lie about your age. *Lucille Ball*
- You can only be prepared for the life you have already lived.
- Failure is not falling down, but staying down.
- Nothing dies quicker than a new idea in a closed mind.
- Don't do things not to die, but to live.

> A good way to learn to be successful is to hang out with successful people. Ask them how they got to be where they are. Most people love to talk about their successes and how they created them.

A Woman in a Man's World
Dorothy Engels-Gulden

Dorothy has been in the real estate brokerage business for both commercial and residential properties since 1969. Her career sales have now topped $1 billion. She is currently President of Gulden Real Estate in Palm Beach, Florida. Her e-mail address is deginc@aol.com. She may also be reached at (561) 655-1460.

If I were to define the guiding principle of my life in one word, that word would be *choices*. My life is a sum of the choices I have made both personally and professionally, from what I chose to do in business to my marriage. I have been blessed with good genes, a loving and wise family, a good head on my shoulders, a tremendous amount of energy, a keen sense of who I am, a never-ending curiosity in people and places and a healthy conscience. All these attributes have served me well for succeeding in what was essentially a man's field of endeavor.

I have worked for and with some of the smartest men and, more importantly, I have learned from them not only about my own business but how to be aggressive without being abrasive.

Generally, men negotiate calmly and patiently with very little emotion. As an example, in 1964 my boss, the chairman of the board of a manufacturing company on Long Island, had as one of his largest investors, the Rockefeller Brothers Foundation. He went to see David Rockefeller for an additional loan of $1 million. (In 1964, a million dollars was worth a lot more than it is today.) We arrived at Rockefeller Center in Manhattan and ascended to one of the top floors of this skyscraper. Once our presence was announced we were escorted into the Rockefeller boardroom. I remember the size and grandeur of the room. I felt like a midget in a castle. The very long boardroom table was made of a single piece of wood. There seemed to be fifty or sixty wingback chairs flanking the table against a wooden paneled background. At the far end of the room, behind the head of the table, was a massive portrait of John D. Rockefeller, Sr.

I asked my boss, Andre Brault, if he were nervous. His answer was the first of many lessons in my journey. He replied, "Every man puts his pants on one leg at a time. The worst he can say is *no*." Andre asked—and got the commitment. His lesson became invaluable to me throughout my career.

When employers and, later, clients of mine succeeded in their business and professional lives, I cheered them. I figured if they can do it in this land of opportunity, why couldn't I? I never doubted myself. More importantly, I never considered being a woman an obstacle.

My parents taught me that success is a journey and not an end. One can be successful and not sacrifice morals or a code of ethics. Success can come from dealing honestly and working hard. I have seen fellow real estate brokers succeed with charm, good nature, hard work, confidence and a keen personal sense of self-esteem. I've seen others without these qualities also prevail in this business, but with little respect or friendship from their colleagues.

Even though my background was not unusual, I was given opportunities that did not exist for my mother, let alone my grandmothers. At the age of seventeen my grandmother, Annie Hewitt, left her family in Ireland and came to America. She hoped for a better life, even though she knew she would probably never see her family again. With no promises or guaranty, she simply boarded a ship. At a time when Irish Catholics "need not apply," she worked in the governor's mansion in New York City for then governor, Teddy Roosevelt. Originally employed as a domestic, she worked herself up to executive housekeeper of the mansion. This was a very prestigious position for an immigrant, much less a woman. She gave all of that up for marriage, because good girls stayed home and had babies.

My mother was number six of seven. A daughter of Irish immigrants, she completed private high school and then worked as an executive secretary in a large perfume company. Much like her mother before her, she gave up her promising career for marriage and family.

My Mom did not raise me with limitations. I watched her—a wonderful homemaker, wife and mother—achieve her measure of success. She enabled and encouraged all four of her children—myself and three brothers—to reach whatever heights we wanted. There was no different treatment for girl or boy. I had to be equal to any task I was assigned or chose to do.

When my father was instructing the boys; I listened as well. "A man is only as good as his word," he would say. There is no difference in this axiom for women, and I have lived by it all my life. When my Father suggested that the boys go out and play and I stay in to help with chores; my mother would say, "If the boys go out to play, the girl goes out to play. If the girl stays in to help with the chores, the boys remain and help as well."

All three boys turned out to be wonderful fathers, husbands and friends. Each stayed married to his first wife. I went on to become a professional, earning a goodly share of rewards both financial and professional. I married, divorced after fifteen years, and raised a child as a single parent—with all the problems associated with that life style.

Equality helps foster competition. Because of the equality that I experienced in my early home life, the expectation to excel through competition was part of my upbringing. In other words, there were no excuses for failure based on gender. My older brother taught me to play chess at the age of five—for no other reason than that he wanted a playmate. This early introduction into the male prerogative of competition prepared me for the many battles that lay ahead outside my home. My brother always challenged me to be better, not as a female, but as a player.

Women in business do face some significant differences from the road followed by businessmen, however. Most successful male executives have a wife-homemaker. Successful businesswomen need homemakers as well, but this need is often not as easily met. There is a perception today that women can have it all. Sometimes that is true, but I have found some things will go by the wayside if I don't pay enormous attention to the multiple roles I, as a women, presume to carry.

There is a price, and for each of us, it is a different price. For me, it was lost time—time not spent having more children, time not spent in gracious socializing, entertaining, and being entertained. When there is not enough time, all personal relationships suffer. They suffer because of the distractions of business, fatigue, endless phone calls and late nights with clients.

An ambitious businessman is expected to spend long hours at the office and not be distracted by family activities. Businesswomen are expected to be there for their children's homework, little league practice and doctors' appointments. We are expected to shop economically, bring supplies home, put them away, concoct daily menus, prepare delicious meals, serve them invitingly—and then clean up. We are expected to call family friends to schedule convenient dinner parties and arrange social engagements. We are the ones who must remember to send cards on all occasions and play Santa 52 weeks a year. It is the women who always seem automatically to carry the burden and responsibility for the nest. Women are now lawyers, doctors, astronauts, scientists and politicians—yet they are still responsible in large part for all the nesting.

To convince ourselves that business success and femininity are not an impossible combination, it is important to look for strong role models. As a real estate broker, I have been privileged to meet some female trail-blazers. One was the late Florence Baumritter, one of the first female lawyers in New York. She had gone to law school with Bella Abzug at a time when men made it very, very difficult for a woman. Another was Ella Scher, who was the first female criminal attorney in New York City. Then there was Meg Kramer, a chemist, who created thirteen patents for allergy products while directing the New York University Medical Center's Allergy Department. These exceptional women had long marriages to supportive, intelligent men who encouraged them. Two of them had children and raised them successfully as well. All three were inspirations for me. What did these dynamic women have to prove? All came from privileged families. All were, obviously, very smart. What hurdles men must have thrown in their paths to keep them from becoming successful!

I recall a story that Mrs. Baumritter told. She, Bella Abzug and another female classmate were shunned and ignored by the rest of their male law school classmates because they were invading male turf. They were women in a world that had been exclusively male. They believed that they alone deserved the education and the jobs that would inevitably follow. Times have changed. Today my daughter is in law school with approximately a 50:50 ratio of women to men.

Women have been making huge strides and, thus, opening many new avenues. Amelia Earhart, Geraldine Ferraro, Sally Ride and now Eileen Collins, the first female commander of a spacecraft, have made and are making history.

A woman in a man's world is no longer the exception. I will not go so far as to say it has become or is becoming the rule, but we are gaining every day. We are graduating more professional women from our universities and, in some universities, more women than men. The future is bright, hopeful and promising. We have little to hold us back other than our own fear.

In the past, the price of being successful women was considered to be losing our femininity, our love lives and our families. Hopefully, this is over. My daughter's future is brighter because my generation helped make it so. Entrepreneurial pursuits are the fastest growing avenues of business for women today, and revenues from women-owned businesses have doubled since 1992.

What do men bring to business that women do not? There is a presumption (perhaps instilled by our mothers and grandmothers) that men are more apt leaders than are women. Men with their commanding size and voices find it easier to get attention when it is needed. Women can have a more challenging time commanding the instant respect that men in comparable roles seem to achieve effortlessly. But it can be done. My voice is not powerful and can be husky, but a softer voice can be overcome with good eye contact and a command of the subject. Eye contact is one of the most important keys to success for a businesswomen. Make good eye contact when you shake someone's hand.

A woman must learn that her conversation must be to the point, especially in a business environment. If she has nothing to add, she should keep quiet. I think this is hard to learn for most women who are conditioned to believe the burden to make conversation in social settings is on them. In business, however, it is the opposite. Social chatter can actually work against everything you are trying to do. Being quiet is not unfeminine. It is more important as a professional to know what you are talking about than to keep the conversational ball rolling. Knowledge is everything in business. Read everything you can about your field of endeavor to stay in front of the information curve.

With the internet and information technology racing at its current pace, it is performance that counts. To reach our goals, we each must learn to work more effectively. The right of women to strive to achieve has already been won for us in the 1960's thanks to Steinham, Abzug, Freidan, *et al*. Women threw down the gauntlet saying we could be more than kitchen aids, bedroom mates and child bearers for our men. We said there was more to life for us than *Leave It To Beaver, Ozzie and Harriet* or *Father Knows Best*. We looked to the few that went before and said there could be many to come. At least this woman did. I sometimes have thought that we actually liberated the men by taking on the tremendous burden to have these careers. Honestly, though, it's been very rewarding.

After some five years of owning my own business and accomplishing some startling deals with respect to the local real estate market, I was asked to join the advisory board of a Palm Beach bank. At the very first meeting, I entered the boardroom with trepidation. I had reached a level of success in my business and in the community, but this was my first experience with an all-male board. In spite of all my confidence, this was still daunting. It made sense from a business perspective, since most of the members were lawyers, real estate developers and investors—but all were men. However, I was very quick to learn that it was what one brought to the meeting, not one's gender, was what counted. The ideas for better bank performance, increasing deposits, improving good will in the community and advancing the other issues banks must deal with in a community were what counted. The men probably felt awkward as they cleaned up their language, but they respected performance, and I performed the duties assigned to me successfully. The nervousness of that first meeting and working with men at that level soon wore off, and we became a team.

In retrospect, if I had it all to do over again, would I pursue a life as a business professional? I paid a price, of course. I divorced for other reasons, but I can say the long hours I devoted to business took time from the family, and that did not help an already strained relationship. Perhaps if I had been more certain of my goals at the time, I'd have chosen a different partner. My time spent away from home in meetings with clients, out of town or otherwise, related to the business took time away from watching my child grow and mature. I would have like to have stayed at home longer, but I couldn't do that and keep a career on track. In most businesses, you lose your contacts and referral base quickly when you take an extended leave.

I was fortunate that I could, to some extent, establish some of my own hours. I took my daughter to school every morning until she went to boarding school in her junior year in high school; so she only missed me between the end of school hours and sleep time. Although I generally work six days a week, I always tried to keep Sundays for myself, my family and church.

The price of success is directly related to what a woman is willing to sacrifice. Would I do it all again? Would I make the same decisions? I think I would. Perhaps my only regret is that I did not have more children, but there again, my life would have been very different.

If I were to give advice to bright young women, my advice would be simple. Just do it. Fearing to begin is the enemy. Take baby steps, if you must, but start. Pretty soon these baby steps will turn into strides and leaps. The first foot forward is always the hardest. Above all, take pride in being motivated and smart. Accept the challenge and go for it. The world is yours for the taking.

> A person who really wants to do something, finds a way.
> Others merely find an excuse.

LIKE MONEY IN THE BANK

Imagine that there is a bank that credits your account each morning with $86,400. It carries over no balance from day to day. Every evening the bank deletes whatever part of the balance you failed to use during the day. What would you do? Draw out every cent, of course!
 Each of us has such a bank. Its name is TIME. Every morning, time credits you with 86,400 seconds. Every night it writes off, as lost, whatever part of this time you have failed to invest to good purpose. It carries over no balance. It allows no overdraft. Each day it opens a new account for you. Each night it burns the remains of the day. If you fail to use the day's deposits, the loss is yours.
 There is no going back. There is no drawing against tomorrow. You must live in the present on today's deposits. Invest it so as to get from it the utmost in health, happiness, and success! The clock is running. Make the most of today. Do something nice for someone.

- To realize the value of ONE YEAR, ask a student who failed a grade.
- To realize the value of ONE MONTH, ask a mother who gave birth to a premature baby.
- To realize the value of ONE WEEK, ask the editor of a weekly newspaper.
- To realize the value of ONE HOUR, ask the lovers who are waiting to meet.
- To realize the value of ONE MINUTE, ask a person who missed the train.
- To realize the value of ONE SECOND, ask a person who just avoided an accident
- To realize the value of ONE MILLISECOND, ask the person who won a silver medal in the Olympics.

 Treasure every moment that you have! And treasure it more because you shared it with someone special, special enough to spend your time. And remember that time waits for no one. Yesterday is history. Tomorrow is mystery. Today is a gift. That's why it's called the present!

CHAPTER SEVEN

HEALTH—RISK AND OPPORTUNITY

It is easier to focus on your growth as a human being if you are strong and in good health. Even worrying about your health can drain your emotional and spiritual batteries. This chapter presents a number of health and fitness topics that are important for midlife women. The following overview will help you understand what you can do to make the most of your mind-body alignment.

MENOPAUSE MADE EASY

A lot of myths surround *the change*. What is really going on, and when and how does it happen? Menopause is a natural condition marking the end of fertility. It literally means the cessation of menstruation. Menopause is considered *official* when a woman hasn't had a menstrual period for 12 consecutive months. For most American women, this happens between the ages of 45 and 55; but it also can come as early as the thirties and as late as the sixties. The natural approach to menopause involves looking at it not as a disease to be treated, but as a positive transition into the next phase of life.

Do you have PMZ? No, not PMS—that's premenstrual syndrome. PMZ is a liberation, not liability. PMZ stand for postmenopausal zest, a phrase coined by anthropologist Margaret Mead. What she meant was that women should seize this stage of life and live it to the fullest. Postmenopausal women are unencumbered by contraception and pregnancy and that once-a-month cycle that used to slow them down. This, she said, is freedom.

"It's a time for exploring what it feels like to be a woman in the human sense, not just as someone who raises children," says Irene Simpson, a naturopathic practitioner in Arlington, Washington. "My friends and I are on the verge of menopause and we are finding it very empowering. We are finding personal growth at a time when women used to decline."

Education about physiological changes and an adventurous outlook can make a big difference in handling the stresses that come with menopause, as well as the life changes (children moving out, parents moving in, for example) that many women are faced with in their late forties and early fifties. Make changes in your life for the better, says Simpson. Go back to school, find a new hobby, take charge of your own health. Make life an adventure!

Perimenopause happens about three to five years before a woman's last period, usually in her forties. Hormone levels may decrease in an erratic manner, causing irregular menstrual cycles and heavy bleeding. Some women find that their cycles get shorter, others that they lengthen.

Menopause marks a dramatic decline in sex hormones, notably estrogen. Estrogen is produced mainly in the ovaries from the time a girl goes through puberty until menopause. Estrogen builds up the lining of the uterus. After menopause, the adrenal glands continue to pump out an estrogen precursor called androstenedione, which is converted in fat cells into a less powerful form of estrogen called estrone. Symptoms of this estrogen decline can be irregular periods, PMS, hot flashes, mood changes, disrupted sleep, vaginal dryness, incontinence, memory changes and decreased concentration.

Two other hormones are also involved. Progesterone, secreted by the ovaries and the adrenal glands, triggers the sloughing off of the uterine lining when fertilization hasn't occurred. After menopause, only very small amounts of progesterone are produced.

Testosterone—an androgen, or male sex hormone, thought to drive libido—is produced by the adrenal glands and the ovaries in pre-menopausal women. With menopause, testosterone levels fall also.

Menopause can bring with it an increased risk for osteoporosis and coronary heart disease. Nowadays a woman can expect to live about one-third of her life after menopause. Coronary heart disease is the number one killer of women over 45. Every year about 233,000 women die from heart disease, and the risk rises with age. A woman's risk increases dramatically after menopause because of the decrease in estrogen production. Estrogen has a protective effect on the heart, lowering the *bad* LDL cholesterol while raising the *good* HDL cholesterol, stimulating blood circulation, and keeping the coronary arteries open.

SELF CARE

Lifestyle changes can help relieve hot flashes and other symptoms. You have probably heard this advice before—stop smoking, exercise regularly, eat right and reduce stress. Here is why these recommendations are so important during menopause.

Stop smoking. Cigarette smoking is known to increase a woman's risk of heart disease and osteoporosis, and menopausal women are already at risk for both diseases because of reduced estrogen levels.

Exercise. Women who are active seem to experience fewer hot flashes. As a woman gets older, she should pay attention to two particular types of exercise: weight-bearing exercise, such as strength training, which helps slow bone loss, and aerobic exercise, such as walking or swimming, which can lower the risk of developing heart disease. To keep bones strong, work your way up to 30 minutes of weight training twice a week. The North American Menopause Society advocates at least 30 minutes of moderate aerobic exercise every day. This can be as simple as walking quickly for two miles.

Anticipate hot flashes. Dress in layers and choose natural fibers over synthetic ones. During a hot flash, think *cool*.

Find a cool spot if possible and drink a cool beverage, or take a cool shower. At night, make sure your bedroom is cool. Eat small meals. Rather than loading your system three times a day, eating five or six small meals will help regulate your body's temperature.

Control your weight. Being overweight puts you at increased risk for heart disease, arthritis, and diabetes. It is not only excess weight that matters, but where you carry that extra weight. Fat around the waist and stomach is particularly dangerous for your heart.

Eat a healthy diet. In 1900, menopausal women could count on about five more years of life. Today they can look forward to 25 to 30 years or more. Eating right is always important, but it can become more difficult as you reach menopause. Because of a slowing of metabolism, you have to get more nutritional punch for your calories, or you are likely to gain weight. Choose lower fat meat and dairy products, and eat lots of fruits and vegetables.

Make sure you get enough calcium and vitamin D, as a way to help stave off osteoporosis. Women on estrogen replacement therapy are advised to ingest 1,000 milligrams of calcium a day. Women not on such a regimen are advised to raise that amount to 1,500 milligrams. The best sources of calcium are low fat dairy products such as cheese, yogurt and milk because they contain vitamin D and lactose, two substances that aid calcium absorption. Calcium is also available in canned fish such as salmon and sardines, dark-green leafy vegetables such as kale, collard and broccoli, and calcium-fortified foods such as some orange juices and breads made with calcium-fortified flour.

Vitamin D is needed for calcium absorption. The best natural food sources are fish oils, butter, cream, egg yolk and liver. Milk is the only food fortified with appreciable amounts of vitamin D. Getting about 10 to 15 minutes of sunlight two to three times a week can also meet your vitamin D needs.

Your need for iron may increase around the time of menopause if you have heavy menstrual periods. If you feel fatigued and have a history of anemia, you may need iron. Make sure you consult your doctor if you are concerned.

Some researchers believe that women would be less prone to menopausal symptoms if their diets restricted meat, kept fat to under 20 percent of their calorie intake, ate lots of fruits, vegetables and whole grains, and included at least one serving a day of tofu or a soy food.

Soy contains naturally occurring chemicals called phytoestrogens (plant estrogens), which the body converts into hormone-like substances. These phytoestrogens are thought to have the same beneficial effects as estrogen and offer another way to combat menopausal symptoms as well as potentially reduce the risk of developing breast cancer, heart disease and osteoporosis. Foods believed to contain phytoestrogens include oilseeds, particularly flaxseed oil and soybeans. Here is some good advice for using phytoestrogens. Have a half-cup of tofu or one cup of soy milk per day. Sprinkle a couple tablespoons of soy nuts or ground flaxseed on your cereal or salads to boost your phytoestrogen level.

Some foods are known to induce hot flashes. These include caffeine, alcohol, spicy foods, hot drinks and chocolate. You might find it helpful to avoid them.

Drink plenty of water. Eight gasses of water is recommended to help your body function best. Buy a large plastic bottle of water—or fill your own—and make yourself finish it by the end of the day.

Take supplements. Certain vitamin and herbal supplements can help relieve menopausal symptoms. Talk to your doctor about what would be effective for you. Some women swear by B-vitamin complexes as a way to help fight dry skin and hair. Others find that vitamin E taken orally (200 to 600 IU per day) can help relieve hot flashes and vaginal dryness. Vitamin E is present in vegetable oils, brown rice, wheat germ and nuts.

Herbs such as wild yam root, ginseng, peppermint tea, and the Chinese herb *Dong Quai* are said to relieve some menopausal symptoms. Make sure you consult a licensed naturopath or a doctor conversant with such supplements before starting on a regiment of vitamin or herbal supplements.

Reduce stress. Stress creates havoc on your health. Along with physical changes that are occurring in your body during menopause, other life changes coincide to bring on new stresses for you to deal with. Learning to cope with this stress can help your well-being. Some options for stress reduction include massage, exercise, meditation and yoga. Give them a try and see which works best for you. The benefits can be astounding.

Stay sexy. Research shows that women having intercourse on a regular basis (once a week or more) have fewer or no hot flashes compared to women who have sporadic sex. They found that frequent sex helps moderate the dropping estrogen levels, which in turn indirectly stimulates failing ovaries. This helps moderate the hormonal system and prevents extreme swings in the estrogen level.

Alternative solutions for menopausal symptoms

Women are now looking to supplements and herbs, not synthetic hormones to ease the body through this sometimes-tricky transition. There are natural approaches for health and balance. Read on for an introduction to some of the most effective ones; then find some good books to learn more about the therapies that interest you.

Aromatherapy. A good reference book is *Aromatherapy; Applications and Inhalations* by herbalist Jeanne Rose. Rose states that clary sage essential oil, used in a home diffuser, may help ease hot flashes. For portable relief carry a handkerchief scented with clary sage and inhale it whenever you feel a flush coming on. Keep the handkerchief in a plastic bag so the smell doesn't dissipate.

Ayurveda. For hot flashes, David Frawley, director of the American Institute of Vedic Studies, recommends swallowing a teaspoon or two of aloe vera gel before meals and before going to bed at night.

Flower Remedy/Essence Therapy. Susan Lange, O.M.D., suggests the flower essence of Aloe Vera.

Herbal Therapy. This therapy is one of the safest and most potent ways to support your body and allow it to make the hormones it needs. As an example, scientific studies conducted in Europe show that the herb black cohosh relieves hot flashes.

Homeopathy. The Family Guide to Homeopathy by Andrew Lockie, M.D. gives many choices for the ease of menopausal symptoms.

Reflexology. You may help control hot flashes by working the diaphragm, reproductive system, pituitary, thyroid and adrenal gland reflexes on your feet, says reflexologist Dwight Byers author of *Better Health with Foot Reflexology.*

Relaxation and Meditation. Slow deep breathing may reduce the number and severity of hot flashes by calming the central nervous system. Practice deep breathing twice a day for 15 minutes as a preventive measure—or use it when you feel a flash coming.

Hormone replacement therapy

Hormone replacement therapy (HRT) is a prescription drug therapy consisting of estrogen and progestin, two female hormones that a woman's body stops producing at menopause. It is a way to ease menopausal symptoms and a way to prevent chronic disease. HRT can prevent—but not reverse—the bone loss that can contribute to osteoporosis. It can also *increase* the risk of clots in the veins and lungs. HRT may also increase the risk of breast cancer. Estrogen given without progestin—called estrogen replacement therapy—raises the risk of uterine cancer.

Although millions of women follow a regimen of HRT, it is not the right choice for every woman. Each woman must look closely at her own personal and family medical background. Most doctors will prescribe hormone therapy to women who have undergone surgical menopause before age 45. These women will live longer without the benefits of natural estrogen and so will have higher risks of heart disease and osteoporosis. Other women who may benefit are those at high risk of fractures because of long term oral steroid use, as well as those for whom quality of life is being adversely affected by menopausal symptoms. If a woman has heart disease, high blood pressure, diabetes, liver disease, blood clots, seizures, migraine headaches, gallbladder disease or a history of cancer, she may not be the best candidate for HRT.

If you decide in favor of HRT, the regimen can be personalized in terms of dosage, type and frequency for your individual needs. Complete the *self-assessment worksheet* and look at the *decision chart* you will find later in this chapter. Take them with you to discuss the possible benefits, risks and side effects with your doctor. Let your doctor know all the prescription drugs you are taking, as well as any nutritional supplements or herbs you are using. Be sure to ask your doctor the following questions:

- What do you think are my long-term health risks based on my personal and family medical histories?
- What are the reasons I should start HRT now rather than waiting until later in life?
- Do you advise estrogen alone or in combination with progestin? Why?
- What form of HRT—pill, patch, ring—do you recommend and why?
- What kinds of side effects should I expect?
- Are there any side effects that warrant immediate medical attention?
- How long will I need hormone replacement therapy?
- If I opt for HRT, what kind of regular follow-up care do I need?

Osteoporosis—Are You at Risk?

Women develop less bone mass than men. Then, for several years after menopause, women also lose bone at an increased rate because their bodies are producing less estrogen. Most people reach their peak bone mass in the spine between the ages of 25 and 30 and reach their peak bone mass in the long bones—such as the femur—from age 35 to 40. After a person passes this peak bone mass age, and especially after about age 45, all the bones in the body begin to lose density. Because osteoporosis is difficult to detect in early stages, it is important to determine your risk well before you have lost much bone mass. Official diagnosis of osteoporosis often comes too late—after a fracture. According to Kenneth Cooper, M.D., in his book *Preventing Osteoporosis*, the strategy must be to start fighting bone loss early and never to let up.

The following list will help you to measure your risk factors. How many of these statements are true of you?

- Have a family history of osteoporosis or other bone disease.
- Are Caucasian and with ancestors from Europe or the Far East.
- Have a fair complexion.
- Have a small-boned frame.
- Have a low percentage of body fat.
- Are more than 40 years old.
- Have had your ovaries removed.
- Have never had children.
- Have gone through early menopause.
- Are allergic to dairy products—or have a low calcium diet.
- Have a sedentary lifestyle.
- Smoke cigarettes.
- Drink alcohol regularly.
- Have malabsorption problems.
- Use or have used steroid-based medications (for example, cortisone and prednisone), anticonvulsants (such as, Dilantin), or thyroid hormone for a long period of time.

Symptoms of osteoporosis are back pain, height loss, curving spine, broken bones, rib pain, abdominal pain, breathing problems and tooth loss. Not long ago, it was impossible to diagnose osteoporosis until a bone fractured. Now, with better x-ray techniques, it can be identified in terms of bone mass. Bone density varies throughout the body, and different measurement techniques give different results, so there is no absolute standard defining what is healthy. The World Health Organization has proposed a system based on relative values; that is, it set the average bone density for women in their thirties as the healthy norm. This is when bone mass is typically at its peak.

A medical evaluation for osteoporosis includes a physical exam, in which height and weight are measured and a check is made for pain or bone deformities. Tests for thyroid function and bone levels of vitamin D may be included as well. But the only way to accurately measure bone health is with a bone density test.

A bone density test involves a scanner that uses a small amount of radiation to measure bone density. The most exact way to measure bone density in the wrist, hip and lower spine is with dual energy x-ray absorptiometry (DEXA). Very low bone mass at any place in the body is a good indicator that osteoporosis affects the entire body.

How often a woman should be tested after menopause hasn't been determined. Some experts recommend testing every four years if your bones are fine. If your bones are at risk, they suggest testing every year. For the density testing center nearest you, call the National Osteoporosis Foundation's action line at 1-800-464-6700.

In addition, blood and urine tests can help determine how rapidly old bone is being removed and new bone being formed, as well as identify possible causes of bone loss. These tests measure proteins that are in the framework of bone or proteins that are necessary for bone formation. However, they don't indicate how much bone mass a person has, and so do not provide the information needed to determine whether to take preventive steps. Blood and urine tests only indicate whether a person is responding well to treatment for osteoporosis.

Ways to stronger bones

If you don't exercise, you lose bone mass. A number of studies support the theory that weight-bearing exercise can actually increase bone mass. Even walking helps your bones, and it is a safe way to get your bones the exercise they need. Walk at least 20 minutes a day, three or four days a week.

Some scientists believe that a chronic shortage of dietary calcium is a contributing factor in developing osteoporosis. Low-fat cheese and yogurts are high in calcium. Skim milk offers the same calcium as regular milk without the fat. Other high-calcium foods include salmon, sardines, nuts and tofu.

Calcium supplements can work small wonders. Calcium carbonate is well absorbed in the stomach by most people. It is typically the least expensive source and offers the highest amount of calcium per tablet. Ask your doctor if a supplement program would benefit you.

Vitamin D is essential to calcium absorption. First, it increases absorption of calcium in the intestines and, second, it increases re-absorption of calcium through the kidneys.

Here are some quick tidbits of information you should know. Alcohol reduces bone formation. Smoking reduces estrogen levels. Dietary protein increases calcium excretion more than it increases calcium absorption, therefore excessive protein in your diet can lead to an overall loss of calcium from the body. A high-fiber diet may bind calcium in the stomach. Ingest fiber in moderation. Put down the salt shaker. The more sodium you excrete, the more calcium you excrete.

Using these facts as a guide can help you have and keep strong bones—and live a healthier life.

Self-Assessment Worksheet

To assess your disease risk, complete the worksheet by putting a check next to any true statement.

Heart disease

Risk factors you can't change

☐ I have diabetes.

☐ I have a parent who had a heart attack before age 61.

Risk factors you can change.

☐ My total blood cholesterol is greater than 200 milligrams, or your doctor has told you that you have high blood cholesterol.

☐ My HDL level (good cholesterol) is less than 35 milligrams.

☐ I smoke cigarettes.

☐ My blood pressure readings are consistently about 140/90, or your doctor has told you that you have high blood pressure.

☐ I am more than 30 percent overweight, and your extra fat has settled around your waist, not your hips and thighs.

Osteoporosis

Risk factors you can't change

☐ I reached menopause before age 45.

☐ I am of Caucasian or Asian descent.

☐ I am thin or have a small build.

☐ I have a family history of osteoporosis.

Risk factors you can change

☐ I smoke cigarettes.

- ☐ I have one or more drinks of alcohol a day.
- ☐ I don't get much exercise.
- ☐ My diet isn't very high in calcium.

Breast Cancer

Risk factors you can't change

- ☐ I have a mother or sister who got breast cancer before menopause.
- ☐ I have never had children.
- ☐ I have atypical hyperplasia (your breast cells are both abnormal and increased in number.) This is more important if you have a family history of breast cancer.
- ☐ I have benign breast disease with hyperplasia (excessive growth of cells.)
- ☐ My first pregnancy was after age 30.
- ☐ I started menstruating before age 12.
- ☐ I reached menopause after age 55.

Risk factors you can change

- ☐ I have one or more drinks of alcohol a day.
- ☐ I am overweight, and your extra fat has settled around your waist, not your hips or thighs.

Use the following chart to help you work with your doctor to examine your personal risks and benefits for hormone replacement therapy (HRT)

Hormone Replacement Therapy	
Known benefits: • Relieves hot flashes • Relieves vaginal dryness and soreness • Reduces insomnia or irritability (if caused by interrupted sleep from night sweats) • Reduces bone loss	**Known risks:** • Increases risk of endometrial cancer (estrogen alone) • Can increase the risk of gallstones • Can increase the risk of fibroid tumors
Suspected benefits: • Reduces risk of heart disease • Reduces risk of stroke • Reduces risk of endometrial cancer (estrogen plus progestin) • Tempers mood swings • May help prevent or reduce the severity of Alzheimer's disease	**Suspected risks:** • May aggravate seizures, asthma, migraines, diabetes and liver disease • May cause blood clots • May slightly increase the risks of breast cancer
Consider HRT if: • You want to alleviate menopausal symptoms • You are at higher than average risk of osteoporosis • You have no previous history of heart disease but are at higher than average risk • You have undergone surgical menopause	**Think twice if:**[*] • You have breast cancer or are at higher than average risk • You have heart disease, high blood pressure, diabetes, blood clots, seizures, migraine headaches, gallbladder disease, or a history of breast or uterine cancer • You are experiencing abnormal vaginal bleeding • Your mother took DES (diethylstilbestrol) during pregnancy

---

[*] These situations are not absolute contraindications to HRT but require closer monitoring. For women in these situations, the estrogen patch may be a better option than pills.

Seven Steps to an Energy Overhaul

Here is a basic regimen that will make you strong. Do these seven exercises twice a week, and you will get stronger, build muscle mass and burn more calories even when sleeping. This routine will give you a significant energy boost. With the exercises below, do two sets of eight to twelve repetitions, in some cases, that means eight to twelve per side.

Arms. Sit in a sturdy, stable, armless chair with feet shoulder-width apart, and your arms hanging down. Hold the weights alongside the chair, parallel to your body. Bending your arm at the elbow, lift the weight almost to the shoulder. While lifting, rotate the palm so that it faces your shoulder at the finish. Slowly return the weight to your side and repeat. To save time, lift with both arms at the same time.

Shoulders. Sit leaning forward slightly with your back straight and shoulders relaxed. Your feet should be flat on the ground, shoulder-width apart. Hold weights in both hands with arms down, elbows slightly bent. Slowly raise your arms out to your sides to shoulder level or slightly higher, while keeping your back and shoulders relaxed but fixed throughout. Then slowly lower and repeat.

Hips and rump. Standing with weights cuffed to your ankles, bend forward at the waist up to about 45 degrees and take hold of the back of the chair. Lift one leg behind you as high as possible without strain, bending your knee only slightly. Slowly lower your leg and repeat, switching legs with every motion.

Legs. With weights strapped to your ankles, stand with your feet a few inches apart, holding the back of the chair for balance. Keeping one leg still, slowly raise the lower part of the other leg behind you until the heel is as close to your rear as possible. Slowly lower your leg to the starting position and repeat. Finish a full set with one leg before you switch legs.

Thighs. With weights around your ankles, slide back in a chair until the backs of your knees are against or close to the seat edge. Place a rolled-up towel under your knees to lift them slightly. Let the balls of your feet graze the floor. Extend one leg in front of you until the leg is straight. If necessary, gently hold the sides of the chair to stabilize yourself as you lift. Slowly lower your leg until your foot touches the floor, then repeat, switching legs with each motion.

Back. Lie on your stomach with a pillow under your hips and your arms lying on the floor beyond your head. To anchor your feet, it can help to leave the weights on your ankles. Slowly lift your trunk four to five inches off the floor, keeping your spine rigid. Hold for a second, then slowly lower yourself to the floor. When you can easily do this exercise twelve times; add repetitions to keep adding strength.

Abdomen. Lie on your back with knees bent and feet flat on the floor about twelve inches apart. Place your palms on your thighs. Lift your shoulders off the floor, gently tucking your chin toward your chest as you go. Stop halfway to the sitting position, hold for a moment, and then slowly lower your trunk and head to the ground. When it becomes easy to do twelve repetitions, do more.

AGING AND REPRODUCTION
Randy S. Morris, M.D.

Randy S. Morris, M.D., a Reproductive Endocrinologist, is Associate Clinical Professor of obstetrics and gynecology at University of Illinois Medical School in Chicago, Illinois. He is also Director of the Oocyte Donation Program at The Center for Human Reproduction in Chicago. His areas of expertise (and research) include advanced laparoscopic fertility surgery, in-vitro fertilization (IVF), oocyte donation, intracytoplasmic sperm injection (ICSI), polycystic ovary syndrome (PCOS), and ovarian hyperstimulation syndrome (OHSS). He may be contacted at the Edward Hospital Fertility Center, 801 S. Washington St., Naperville, IL 60540. Phone: (630) 355-0450. Email: editor@infertilitynews.com. Website: www.infertilitynews.com.

The largest number of births ever in the United States occurred in the post World War II "baby boom" between 1947 and 1965. Women born during this time period began reaching the age of 35 in 1982 and will continue hitting that milestone until the end of the century. As a result, during this time period—1982 to 2000—there have been and will be an unprecedented number of women in their late child bearing years.

In addition, many women have decided for various reasons to delay childbearing. This is a significant change from the patterns of previous generations, and it means that more couples will be seeking pregnancy after the age of 35. Furthermore, these couples also have a desire to complete their families in a shorter period of time.

Decline of fertility with age

Although there is still some disagreement over the issue, most fertility experts now agree that fertility decreases with age. There are several pieces of evidence that point to this fact. Some of the most interesting studies involve a religious group known as the Hutterites.

The Hutterites migrated to the U.S. from Switzerland in the 1870s and now live in the Dakotas, Montana and parts of Canada. They are believers in large families and condemn the use of any form of contraception. They also marry only within their own group, and, since they live in a set geographic area, they are relatively easy to investigate.

For these reasons, they make ideal candidates to study the effects of aging on reproduction. It was found that the fertility rate (the number of women achieving a pregnancy per 100 women) is much higher in younger women (twenties) than in older women (forties). After a pregnancy is delivered, it is the Hutterites' practice to immediately attempt to achieve pregnancy again. However, it was noted that the time between pregnancies became increasingly longer with the increasing age of the women studied. The average age at the time of the last pregnancy was 40.9 among Hutterite women—a much higher age than in the general population.

Other data also support the notion that fertility decreases with age. Compared with younger women, women over the age of 35 seek evaluation for infertility twice as often. Some investigators have suggested that this decline is due to a decreased frequency of intercourse in older couples.

For this reason, investigators in France studied the fertility rate among women who were attempting to become pregnant in a donor insemination program because their own partners had no sperm. In this way, the frequency of intercourse did not interfere with calculations of fertility. As expected, the fertility rate dropped significantly after the age of 30 and again after the age of 35. Another similar study suggested that the probability of having a baby decreased 3.5 percent per year after the age of 30.

Increased risk of miscarriage with age

In addition to the lower chance of becoming pregnant, as women age they also have a higher chance of losing the pregnancy (miscarriage). What are the reasons for this? To explain, it is necessary to discuss some aspects of genetics.

Health — Risk and Opportunity

We basically all start out when our father's sperm fertilizes our mother's egg. We can have the characteristics of both our parents. These characteristics are coded in a special way and are found in the structures known as chromosomes.

In fact, the information found on these chromosomes contains all the information about every part of us. The sperm and egg each contain half of the chromosomes necessary to make a complete human being. Simply stated, the process of making sperm and eggs is nothing more than the packaging of different combinations of chromosome so that they can be *mixed* together with another egg or sperm to make different varieties of humans.

Women are born with all the eggs that they will ever have in their lives (with the chromosomes inside). Men, on the other hand, make fresh sperm continuously throughout their whole lives. It takes approximately 90 days for a sperm to be made and to reach maturity. This is an extremely important difference between the sexes because, for example, if a 35 year old man and a 35 year old woman attempt to achieve a pregnancy, they are basically trying to combine a 35 year old egg with a 3 month old sperm. The longer an egg sits around in the ovary, however, the more likely it is to develop abnormalities in its chromosomes. If an egg with abnormal chromosomes is fertilized, then the chances are greater that the resulting pregnancy will end in miscarriage.

In fact, chromosomal abnormality is the single most common cause of miscarriage. From many studies, we know that at least half of all miscarriages are due to abnormal chromosomes. A young woman (in her 20s), therefore, has only a 12 to 15 percent chance of having a miscarriage each time she becomes pregnant. A woman in her 40s, however, has a 50 percent risk of miscarriage.

Down's Syndrome and other chromosomal problems

Not every pregnancy in which the embryo has abnormal chromosomes will end in a miscarriage. Some will continue to develop and even result in the birth of a live baby. These babies, however, can have varying problems, including birth defects and mental retardation. Down's Syndrome is the most common problem of this type, but there are others. There is a progressive increase in the risk of birth defects and mental retardation as the mother's age increases. This is all as a result of aging of the eggs.

Why does fertility decrease?

Until recently, it was not known why fertility decreases with age. One thing was known for sure and that was that the age of the male partner didn't seem to matter much. Even men in their 70s still seemed to be able to produce pregnancies. The Bible carries stories of men in their 90s fathering children. In women, however, the likelihood of a pregnancy after age 45 is extremely rare.

The next question to answer was, "why?" Research has focused on two areas: aging of the uterus versus aging of the eggs. Until recently there was no way to separate these factors, however, the technology of egg donation has enabled us to look at these factors separately. Egg donation is the process whereby eggs from a young woman can be fertilized and placed into the uterus of an older woman.

If fertility decreases because an older woman's uterus is less capable of carrying a pregnancy, then using younger eggs should not produce very many pregnancies in older women. What we found, however, was exactly the opposite. If you use younger eggs, the rate of achieving pregnancies in older women is very high. In fact, egg donation gives the highest rate of pregnancy that is achievable with any type of fertility treatment.

Women in their forties, fifties, and even sixties can all achieve very high pregnancy rates with egg donation. This is excellent proof that fertility decreases with age due to aging of eggs and their chromosomes. Studies that have removed eggs from the ovaries of older women have shown that a large percentage of them have abnormal chromosomes. There is, therefore, probably a continuum of possible outcomes in chromosomally abnormal eggs. Most will probably not fertilize. Of those that do, many will be lost to miscarriage. A few that remain as viable pregnancies, will end up as a Down's Syndrome or a related chromosomal problem.

"But I had a friend who had a normal baby when she was 46 years old!"

Every human being is different. Not all women will develop abnormalities in their eggs' chromosomes at the same age. And of course, even if a majority of a woman's eggs contain abnormal chromosomes, it only takes one to achieve that *normal pregnancy*. The great majority of women will not be able to become pregnant after age 46. On the other hand, even some younger women may have a rapid decline in the ability of their eggs to produce a pregnancy. Such women often have an early menopause.

Fertility tests and fertility treatments

The most important test we currently have to determine a woman's *ovarian reserve*—that is, the capability of her eggs to be able to produce a pregnancy—is a blood test for follicle stimulating hormone. FSH is made in a gland near the brain, called the pituitary. It is the *key* hormone responsible for the cyclic development of eggs every month.

As a woman's eggs become less capable of producing a pregnancy, the levels of FSH begin to rise. Therefore, as you might expect, FSH generally increases in women as they get older. Women who have gone through menopause have very high levels of FSH (and are incapable of becoming pregnant with their own eggs). However, young women who have had an accelerated decline in the quality of their eggs can also have high FSH levels.

In order to determine a woman's FSH level for the purpose of predicting fertility, the blood should be drawn on the third day of the menstrual cycle. At our laboratory, a normal level for FSH on day three is less than 7 IU. Women with levels between 7 and 12 IU are considered elevated but have been able to achieve pregnancies with us.

Women with levels consistently over 12 IU have an extremely poor chance of pregnancy. In fact, we have had only one woman over the last few years who has gone home with a baby when her FSH level was higher than 12. (It was 14.3.)

Now to add little more complexity: day three FSH levels can vary from month to month and can be affected by such things as estrogen levels. In other words, a high FSH level one month doesn't necessarily mean it will be elevated every month. There is evidence accumulating that, if a woman has levels of FSH that fluctuate greatly, she may have a better chance of achieving a pregnancy in a month when her FSH is lower than in a month when it is very high. Her chance will probably never be as good as in a woman who never has high FSH levels, however.

Unfortunately, there are no treatments available which can *turn back the clock* on a woman's ovaries. Many physicians use fertility medications to try to increase the chance of pregnancy. The idea behind using such medications is to increase the number of eggs that develop in a given month, thus enhancing the chance that at least one of them might be able to be fertilized and develop into a viable pregnancy. This seems to offer some improvement in results, but the pregnancy rates are not as good as in younger women. Also, many women don't respond well to fertility medications as they get older.

Others have advocated in-vitro fertilization (IVF) as a means to achieve pregnancy in such cases. Unfortunately, the pregnancy rates with IVF in women over the age 40 are very low.

Currently, the only consistently successful method to improve pregnancy rates in women with age-related infertility is egg donation. The indications for egg donation include:

1. Age over 40
2. Persistently high FSH levels at any age
3. Poor response to fertility medications at any age
4. Poor egg quality for IVF
5. Age-related recurrent miscarriage

As compared to pregnancy rates of less than 10 percent per cycle for women over the age of forty, egg donation results in pregnancy rates of more than 35 percent per cycle. In addition, the risks of miscarriage and Down's Syndrome are dramatically reduced. Thus the likelihood of *taking home a baby* is very much higher. A recent study presented at the IVF World Congress indicated that after four cycles of egg donation, over 80 percent of women delivered a baby.

Conclusion

Fertility decreases with age. This decrease is most likely due to aging of the eggs and the chromosomes inside them. The risk of miscarriage and delivering chromosomal abnormal babies also increases with age. The most successful method for achieving a pregnancy and taking home a baby as female age advances is with the use of egg donation. If you are interested in egg donation, please contact your physician to determine if this treatment is right for you.

Exercise for Health

Sean Kenny, C.P.T.

Sean Kenny is certified by the American Council on Exercise and is a Master Member of the IDEA Fitness Professionals Association. Sean owns and operates a private training/consultation business and designs, implements and evaluates fitness programs for medical communities. He can be reached at (805) 831-0805 or via e-mail: seank@kem.com. Sean has written the following informative overview about where, how, why and when to exercise.

Fitness over forty

"I don't need to exercise. I'm busy enough with my job, children and home." I hear this constantly when I inquire about the fitness programs of ladies who consult me. While one can be *busy*, it does not necessarily mean you are exercising or *fit*. Another point busy people need to realize is that exercise helps you make more time in your day—not take time from you. Exercise reduces stress, and gives you more energy and clearer thinking. The end result is a much happier, stress-free and productive life.

Now that you have reasons to exercise, how are you going to fit it into your hectic schedule? As a standard precaution, check with your doctor before you begin any exercise regimen.

Cardiovascular training is perhaps the most important piece of the fitness puzzle. It is through cardiovascular training that one strengthens the heart and lungs, increases endurance, stamina and improves body composition by reducing weight. The great thing about cardiovascular exercise is that it can be done almost anywhere and doesn't require equipment. In people's busy schedules, cardiovascular work can come in the form of a quick morning jog, a bicycle ride or simply a brisk walk. In a recent study from Harvard's School of Public Health, women who engaged in a heart pumping, 30-minute daily walk decreased their chance of colon cancer by 50 percent. House cleaning is also a good cardiovascular workout when it is done at a good pace.

The body thrives on consistency. Attempt to do some type of physical activity every day. Any activity that increases the heart rate and sustains it uninterrupted for a minimum of 20 minutes will provide great results if done at least three times per week. The easiest way to determine your optimum heart rate range is to begin by subtracting your age from 220. The result is your maximum heart rate. Now calculate 65 percent and 85 percent of your maximum heart rate to determine your low and high range. This is your training zone. You want to keep your heart rate in this range for at least 20 minutes. Be sure to allow a few minutes before the exercise to slowly increase your heart rate and a few minutes after to slowly decrease it. This is referred to as the warm-up and cool-down part of the program. Light stretching after you exercise not only helps you to improve flexibility, but it also helps relieve muscle stiffness and improve circulation.

Next, consider weight lifting or resistance training as part of your exercise program. Resistance training helps to strengthen skeletal muscle, which in turn helps with everyday chores. Osteoporosis is also a major concern for women over forty. Some studies report bone loss at the rate of one percent for each year after age 35. Resistance training has been proven to significantly strengthen bone. Bones increase in density as a result of the demands that weight bearing exercises place on them.

Did you know that lifting weights could help you lose weight? As far as weight-loss is concerned, weight training can help you there as well. Muscle is metabolically active tissue, which means it is like a furnace. Muscle burns calories around the clock by increasing your metabolism. In fact, for every pound of muscle you add, your body burns an additional 50 to 100 calories daily. This helps the long term weight loss goal of any program. A simple set of 2-, 5-, 8-, and 10-pound dumbbells in would be ideal. If you do not wish to purchase dumbbells, detergent bottles, milk containers full of water (one cup equals two pounds) or soup cans can be used as resistance.

Fitness in your forties and beyond can work if you are willing to make the effort. It may take conscious planning, but the results will last a lifetime. Remember exercise boosts the immune system and increases energy. Arthritis, back pain, hypertension, diabetes and a host of other ailments also respond favorably to exercise. In addition, it builds self-esteem, as it not only helps you look better, but feel better, too.

Why do I need to exercise

Fitness is like a bank account—if you keep taking out without putting any in, soon you'll end up with a zero balance. Research indicates that even mild exercise (for example, a brisk walk twice a week) can have positive effects on cardiovascular systems, muscle strength, endurance, body composition and energy.

Other benefits of exercise include an enhanced immune system, better sleep patterns, increased stamina and reduced stress. Exercise doesn't just make you feel better; it makes you look better too. Many people say they are too busy to exercise, but research shows that exercise increases your energy and reduces stress to allow you to think clearly. This enables you to work more efficiently, allowing you to get more done and to enjoy your free time more.

Keeping heart rates up when temperatures go down

When the cold weather season is upon us, many find it increasingly difficult to muster the motivation needed to exercise outside. During that time of year, an aerobic program can be moved indoors. Treadmills, stair-steppers and stationary bikes are some of the most popular modes of indoor training that can aid in fat-burning, endurance building, and muscle toning. Here is a quick description of what each piece of equipment can do for you.

Treadmills: Walking is ideal for those just starting an exercise program. Some models give you feedback of distance, time, level, calories burned, heart rate and incline. Walking faster or running allows you to further increase your caloric expenditure.

Stair-steppers: These burn a great number of calories and there's no impact on the joints as there is with running since your feet are always in constant contact with the platform.

Stationary Bikes: This mode of exercise is catching on with the *spinning* classes in which you bike with 20 to 30 other people. Biking is a comfortable; non-impact aerobic exercise that almost anyone can enjoy.

These are only a few of the more popular machines. Others are things such as ski-simulators, rowers, and Health Riders. All of these are options for basic cardiovascular training. Here are some guidelines for an effective program.

- Aim for at least 25 minutes, three times per week.
- Stay in your target heart rate range during the session and gradually decrease it towards the end.
- Go longer, not harder—duration is more important then intensity.

Resistance exercise: weight training

Before lifting, always warm-up. This is a great time to perform the cardiovascular component of your program. By increasing the body's core temperature, you not only provide for a safer workout—a warm muscle exhibits greater flexibility—but you can also lift a bit more since a warm muscle contracts with greater force than when it is cold.

Studies indicate that a selection of exercises in three sets of 12 to 15 repetition each is ideal for toning and firming muscles without adding bulk. Three sets of 12 would be done as follows: do 12 lifts of the selected exercise, rest 30 seconds to a minute, do 12 more, rest, then do your last set of movements with a moderate weight. The weight should be heavy enough to feel that you are working by the 10th,

11th and 12th movement, but not so heavy as to compromise proper form or safety.

Get a day of rest in between weight-lifting sessions, as injuries are frequent if the muscles are overused. Use a combination of machines and free-weight in your program. The machines help build strength without the worry of dropping the weight, needing a spotter or finding yourself unable to control the range of motion. After a solid foundation with machines is acquired, free-weight exercises can be introduced. Free-weights involve more muscles due to the balance and greater range of motion that they demand. Studies also show that free-weight exercises stimulate deeper muscle tissue than their machine counter-parts. Some key points to remember:

- Control your breathing. Exhale when you exert force or pressure.
- Form is always more important than weight. If you can't perform the lift correctly reduce the weight and concentrate on strict, clean form.
- Always warm up prior to lifting.

A toning and conditioning program

Chair Squat: Stand with your back against a wall or door and place your feet approximately 15 inches in front of you, and about shoulder width. Now slide down until your thighs are parallel with the floor. Hold this position for a second, and then return slowly to the standing position. Do not lock your knees or bounce at the top. Use smooth, controlled movements. Perform two sets of 15 repetitions. This is great for toning the quadriceps.

Calf Raise: Stand on the edge of a phone book, dictionary or similar object that is about four to six inches high. Place the balls of your feet on the edge and your heels hanging over. Go up on your toes as high as high as you can and still be comfortable, pause and lower your heels towards the floor until you get a comfortable stretch in your calves. Do two sets of 15 repetitions.

Back Row: Put your left hand and left knee on the edge of a bed or low bench while your right leg is planted on the floor. A weight should be in your right hand, which is hanging straight down towards the floor. Keeping your back parallel with the floor, pull the weight straight up to your chest. Hold this for a second (focusing on squeezing your shoulder blades together) and then lower the weight slowly back down. Switch sides and do the same exercise with the other hand. Do two sets with 15 repetitions in each set.

Lateral Raise: Stand straight and hold a weight in each hand while your arms are down at your sides. Keeping your arms fairly straight, lift your arms straight out from your sides until they are parallel with the floor. Pause and repeat. Do two sets of 15 repetitions.

Shrugs: In the same position as the lateral raise, keep the weight as your sides the entire time and simply move your shoulders as if you are trying to touch your ears with them. Don't bend your arms. Do two sets with 15 repetitions.

Chest Press: Lay down on a bench and look up at the ceiling while having a weight in each hand. Begin this exercise with your elbows and hands up near your shoulders. Press the weight straight up towards the ceiling, but do not lock your elbows. Bring the weights back down and repeat. Do two sets with 15 repetitions.

Arm Curl: Standing with a weight in each hand while your arms are straight at your side, curl one weight up towards your chest. Only bend at your elbow, keeping the your upper arm straight at your side. Squeeze your biceps at the top of the movement, then lower the weight. Alternate each arm. Do two sets with 15 repetitions with each arm.

Triceps Kickback: Support yourself in a similar fashion as you did for the back row. Keep your hand with the weight in it close to your chest, keep your elbow high and next to your body. Now extend your arm backwards, bending only the elbow. Focus on squeezing the triceps muscle on the back of your arm. Do two sets of 15 repetitions on each side.

By doing these basic exercises you will start becoming fit and strong. You can then go to classes or hire a trainer to show you variations and to make sure you are doing them with proper form for maximum benefit.

How to choose a health club

Deciding which fitness center to invest your money in is not as easy as it once was. Today, there are more choices, more amenities, more services and virtually unlimited pricing structure within the industry. The first step is to assess your needs. Many membership fees are based on what you use.

Are you going to use one club or all of their 150 locations? Membership for one location is generally considerably less than a full use card. Why pay for all the other locations you don't visit?

What are you looking for as far as service? Most health clubs now offer day care for a minimal hourly fee. If a club has a pool, that usually increases the facilities operating cost due to increased maintenance and liability. This will be reflected in higher monthly fees. Besides personal trainers, some clubs have licensed therapists, chiropractors and even resident physicians. The gyms of the past are being replaced with comprehensive *wellness centers* offering treatment, education and prevention.

After assessing your fitness needs, examine a few clubs. Do they offer what they advertise? If a facility is said to be available 24 hours, is this all week or just on certain days? Are trainers available to help you design structured fitness programs that meet your needs, goals and schedule? Make sure the training staff is degreed or certified from a legitimate organization and not simply given a quick test provided by their employer. Service is the key to keep you coming back. Having the best equipment won't do you any good if no one is there to help instruct you in its proper use.

Most clubs have what is called *prime time*—when club use is at its peak. You need to see how this affects your schedule. Ask for free passes before you join and try the club on the days and times you will be exercising so you can get an idea of the what the facility is like at those times. Look around. A good staff takes pride in their facility, and this should be reflected in its maintenance, cleanliness and overall appearance.

Make a checklist of all your needs and verify everything before you join. If you decide to join, make sure you understand the agreement you will be entering into. Are their hidden processing fees? Can you get passes for friends? Can you terminate the contract if you get sick or move, and if you can, will there be a penalty charge to do it? Do you get a discount if you pay in full as opposed to monthly?

You are now well informed in the basics of the *when, where, why,* and *how* of fitness. Make a commitment today and live all your tomorrows healthy and empowered.

> *Start with what you can do;*
> *don't stop because of what you can't do.*

CHAPTER EIGHT

BECOMING ME

This chapter consists of inspirational stories from and about women who have had challenges in life and how they have overcome them to succeed. You will see in them a spark of courage or commitment that you can apply to your life.

ONCE AND STILL CHAMPION

Trish Falkner

Trish has owned and managed tennis facilities, was director for the Women's Tennis Association, has been selected as the Over-45 Professional Player of the Year by the USPTA and Player of the Year by the Florida Tennis Association, has been the number one player in the USA in her age group for the last four years and is ranked number two in the world among players over 50. Trish can be reached at Triosports@aol.com.

When I was in my twenties, I looked at people who were in their fifties and sixties as if their lives were almost over. I didn't really think about these observations again until I reached the age where I became the one being classified as old.

    I am now in my mid-fifties, an age my mother never saw, as she died from cancer when she was 47. I certainly don't think of myself as old—wiser, maybe, but never old. When I think about her dying at 47, I realize how much of my life I have lived—and how much I have enjoyed living it—after that age.

I have always taken life for granted. I don't mean in a selfish or even naïve way, but more in the way that one takes a close companion for granted. I developed a personality that allowed me to live my life to it's fullest so that, when it was my time to die, I would know that I hadn't left any opportunity unclaimed or any challenge untried.

Being a youth in Australia made it very easy—and not very expensive—to try all sorts of sports, and my parents were extremely supportive both emotionally and economically. I was good at track, swimming, squash and tennis. The more I excelled, the more I wanted to test myself. I liked the feeling of being both mentally and physically exhausted after a great workout or a close match. When I was a teenager, I enjoyed having a purpose, and clearly defined, achievable goals. My parents made it financially possible for me to take the leap from being a good high school amateur athlete to becoming a world ranked international tennis and squash player. My athleticism helped a little, too!

I never encountered any roadblocks—other than my opponents, who sometimes beat me. I never experienced any discrimination because I was a woman. In all my travels, when I was playing the international circuit, I never felt I was held back because I was too young, too inexperienced or female. My racquet did the talking, and the results gave me self-respect and confidence.

Winning or simply playing well is wonderful positive reinforcement to help a person gain confidence and poise. Sports helped me make friends easily, feel socially comfortable and know that I was really good at something. I was never pressured to play or practice. I think that is why I still enjoy playing tennis fifty years later. I played then and continue to play because I love the game.

I met my husband at a tennis tournament. I feel closer to my boys because I was able to play sports with them and they were able to share my enthusiasm for racquet sports. I met most of my close friends through my tennis or squash careers. Some of these people have been my friends for 40 years. Although they live all over the world, we each have a very close bond because of our ties with sports.

My first love has always been squash, however most Americans think of squash as a fall vegetable rather than a fast paced exhilarating racquet sport. Therefore, when I moved to the United States, I turned my energies more toward tennis. I played all the international tournaments and all the Grand Slams. Thanks to tennis, I was able to travel the world for years and meet wonderful and interesting people. After my days of professional competition were over, I took up teaching, imparting tennis knowledge to even the most uncoordinated students. I have been teaching tennis on and off for 35 years now. When I wasn't teaching, I worked as a Tour Director and then as a Marketing Director for the women's professional tennis tour.

In 1987, I left the Women's Tennis Association and formed my own sports marketing company, Triosports International. I wasn't sure what I wanted to do, but I knew that I wanted it to include tennis. After the first year, I owned or operated four of the $150,000 tournaments on the women's tour. I was on the different side of the net, but I was still in the sport. When the Philip Morris company started to pull back their sponsorship of women's tennis, I decided to go back to teaching.

I took a job as tennis director at a very nice, exclusive club in Florida. Initially, I was not very happy, since I felt I had taken a giant step backwards—here I was teaching tennis again. Surely, with my advancing years—I was now 46 years old—I should find a nice cushy desk job. Occasionally, I would rue the day that allowed me to be born 20 years too soon in the world of professional tennis. If I had played at my level in the 1970s and 1980s, I would be sitting back watching my investments and playing exhibitions for large corporations. That was not to be for me, but I did find that I was very happy teaching people how to play good tennis. I still enjoy seeing novice players begin to understand and try to learn more about the complexities of the game.

I truly appreciate teaching women who have taken up the sport of tennis later in life. Many of them have never done anything physically competitive, and for some of them this is the first attempt at a sport—and it is scary for them. I take pleasure in watching their personalities emerge on the court. Novices start out very timid and afraid of failure, then they suddenly find themselves hooked on this great sport, and they cannot get enough. They take lessons, join leagues and even start to enter local tournaments. Suddenly they become dedicated, focused, competitive *tennis nuts*.

I actually enjoy teaching the more uncoordinated students as they try so hard to do it right. I empathize with their struggles to become an athlete or, at the very least, an adequate tennis player. It is almost like watching a child discover something new. After about only three lessons, I can tell which women will turn into these tennis fiends. I really look forward to their lessons. Their dedication and the trust they have placed in me to take them from a clumsy beginner to a smooth, confident tennis player instills in me a respect for what they are attempting. It also makes me remember how fortunate I was to have the talent and the opportunity to learn the sport of tennis as a child.

Many of these women also undergo some incredible physical changes once they start to play more tennis. Their bodies change shape. They become firmer, healthier and more concerned about their overall fitness level. They make new friends, and in many cases their social life begins to revolve around their tennis games and their playing partners.

I remember one student who came to me at the age of 60. She said, "My children all play, and now I want to see if I can learn." She had no athletic talent whatsoever. She had never played any sport, not even in school. It took her almost three months before she could consistently make contact with the ball. She took lessons for three years, and now she plays four times a week. She can hold her own with her children and can feed balls to her grandchildren.

She looks great, and when she steps on the court she seems to take about 10 years off her age.

Women who have never been in competitive environments also learn how to handle defeat, cheating, frustration, anger and disappointment. They see that it is important in doubles play to have a good relationship with their partners. Teamwork and communication is everything. Singles teaches self-confidence. You are out there alone, and you cannot blame anyone but yourself if you play badly.

I also see some women being unable to continue to have fun playing the game. Petty jealousies arise because one player is taking more lessons and learning faster than another. A partner has a bad day, and a match is lost because one of the players stopped being supportive and communicative. One partner is now playing better than her friend and partner, and she doesn't know how to tell her she wants to move on.

Some friendships and even some marriages are sorely tested on the court. Many couples at my club will not play mixed doubles with their spouses as they say it is too taxing. Good men players typically expect too much of their wives, and the women end up in a quivering heap on the sidelines. If the woman is the better player, then the man with a lot of self-esteem problems constantly feels under attack, and consequently may not play very well. In either case, these matches are unpleasant and stressful, and are better not being played.

Playing sports can present physical problems, as well. Irregular menstruation often plagues young female athletes when they train, travel or bulk up. They may experience no periods for months at a time. When they do come, the periods are often very heavy and rather debilitating. Older women are prone to injury if they do not stretch or have weak bones. Many beginners, particularly if they are over the age of 60, do not have good balance. As we get older our eyesight and reflexes begin to fade. Senior players are much more likely to be struck by a misplayed shot—often one hit by their partners!

Older players also have a harder time coming back from injuries or surgeries. Providing players listen to their doctors' orders for restarting a physical activity, I find that having tennis to look forward to often speeds up the healing process. Tennis is also a game in which you can slow yourself down slightly if you are not 100 percent fit. You can still enjoy the game even if you cannot play with full intensity. One of our club members who had major hip replacement surgery plays six times a week. One of my friends on the senior tour has had both hips replaced, and this year she was ranked number one in the 65 and over category in the United States.

I have had two major surgeries. My first, a hysterectomy in 1983 laid me off tennis for about six weeks. The moment I was allowed back on the court, I was there hitting slowly, and it did feel good to be back swinging and chasing down the shots. After about four weeks, I felt that I was almost back to where I was before the surgery. After another four weeks, I felt ten times better than prior to the surgery. I credit most of that to my tennis and only some of it to my doctor.

My greatest test yet occurred in the middle of 1997. I was enjoying my life. I finally had stopped worrying about my kids. I had a great job and I was playing the best tennis of my life. Then I was diagnosed with breast cancer. Even though I had been preparing myself for those words for years because I knew breast cancer was prevalent in my family, when I heard the doctor tell me, I stopped breathing for a second. Luckily, I had done all the right things and had found the lump very early.

I had a partial mastectomy and—again, lucky for me—it was my left breast, so it did not hamper my tennis. I had the surgery on a Friday and by Monday I was back at work. By the following Monday, I was giving lessons again. I looked upon the whole event as if it were a major tennis tournament that I had been preparing for it all my life. I knew what to do and how to beat it, and I wasn't going to lose. I also had a very close friend who helped me through all the down days. She worked hard to make the daily grind of radiation therapy seem like fun and even brought me picnic lunches to eat while I was waiting for my appointments.

I had a world championship that I wanted to play, so I set my sights and hopes on that. I never had any doubts that I would play. I knew I had the best doctors, and I was doing all I could to get well. The day after I finished the radiation treatment, I jumped on a plane for South Africa and the World Veterans Tennis Championships. I didn't win—even though I had match points in the final—but settling for second was nothing compared to what I had conquered earlier that year. I had used my tennis as an instrumental goal to reach for health.

Tennis has been and probably always will be a major influence in my life. It has been my passion, my work, my play, my exercise, and my savior—and sometimes it has been my only outlet when things have gone wrong. Because of sports, I have a lot to be thankful for.

As I move into my senior years, I have slowed down, however. I do take time to notice nature and beautiful sunsets. I do walk on the beach with my dogs. I still am straining to achieve, although, if I were to be honest with myself, I would have to say, "Its okay to stop now, Trish. You have one of the best jobs in the world, and you are number one in your age group in your sport." My kids are successful and happy. I have achieved all my goals, and I am at peace mentally. I have wonderful friends, and I love my life.

Very few people get to say these words: "I am content in all phases of my life," and really mean them. I can, and I have sports to thank for my contentment.

> *Success lies not in achieving what you aim at but in aiming at what you ought to achieve.*

IT HAPPENS

Melissa Applegate

Melissa is a teacher of Egyptian and Tibetan mysticism, shamanic dreamwork, sitting and moving meditation and has offered private ministerial counseling to individuals for the past two decades. She is presently writing her first book, Pathways to Ecstasy: An Exploration of Rational, Shamanic and Spiritual Approaches to Happiness and Well-being. *She can be reached via e-mail at* anzen@concentric.net.

Somewhere around the age of 40 to 50, *it happens*. It happens to every woman, regardless of race, economic status, geographical location or political, social or religious preference. Like birthdays, taxes and death, it is inevitable. It changes the life of the woman experiencing it (as well as the lives of those around her). For some women, it's no big deal; for others, it's a very big deal.

The *it* referred to does not appear on the infamous bumper sticker with the letters *s-h* before it (although the sentiment *it* generates is curiously similar!). It is commonly referred to as *the change of life, midlife crisis* or simply *menopause*. It manifests as a change in, pause of, and ultimate cessation of the menstrual cycle; however, the physical midlife changes to a woman's body are the least of *it*. During this unique time, changes often occur in other areas of a woman's life besides her body, encompassing a broad spectrum (ranging from relationship, career, finances, philosophy, etc.) that may be mild to severe in temperament. The physical symptoms of menopause can be easily corrected by going to a doctor, obtaining a prescription, and taking some medicine. Life changes such as *empty nest syndrome* (when children mature and leave home or a spouse suddenly abandons a long-time marriage) cannot be so readily dealt with. There is no magic pill to fix these traumatic midlife changes. Healing must be self-generated.

Take for example, Carol, a 49 years old divorced mother of one. As she approached menopause, she found herself immersed in a comfortable long-term personal relationship and successful sales career. Life was comfortable, and then, quite suddenly and unexpectedly, "all hell broke loose," as the expression goes.

After traveling to a third world country, she acquired a short-term viral infection that resulted in taking two months' medical leave from her job. Upon return to work, she received the cold shoulder from her boss, intentional dead-end sales leads and subtle but persistent harassment from the boss that left her feeling inadequate, despondent and resentful. During the course of the following year, she tried several avenues of conflict resolution that proved unsuccessful and subsequently resigned. Being forced out of the workplace on terms other than her own resulted in extreme distress that caused her to become ill once again and incapable of returning to work. She resorted to bankruptcy, lost her home and many of her possessions despite a history of impeccable credit. Simultaneously, her son left home to attend college and her long-term boyfriend abandoned the relationship, not wanting the financial and emotional burden of her unfortunate midlife crisis.

"At the time," she said, "I felt life had dealt me an unjust hand. I had always worked hard and competently on the job, paid my bills on time, maintained an orderly home, adored my boyfriend and son, and sincerely believed myself to be a good person. Suddenly, without warning, the whole fabric of my life was pulled out from under me and there was nothing solid to stand on. Job, boyfriend, son, finances, health and home gone—just like that, in one clean sweep—whoosh, gone! And no one seemed particularly sympathetic. As long term friends disappeared one-by-one, I came to the startling realization that the only person I could truly count on was myself."

"Like it or not", she continued, "change was happening. I realized I could be a victim of this change by clinging to fear or I could stop struggling, go with the flow and see where the tide ultimately took me. I examined where I had been, where I wanted to go, assessed my vocational skills, interests and potential opportunities and came to a profound realization: I had fooled myself into believing I was happy with my former life when, in fact, I was very unhappy. I had worked many hard years in the sales industry and although the money was good, the quality of life was not. I was working long hours, bored silly, up to my ears in debt and had no time to enjoy the fruits of my labor. What little free time I had was spent maintaining a home and grounds that were far too large for just one person.

"Furthermore," she confided, "as much as I hated to admit it, I came to the sad conclusion that my personal relationship had also been stale and stagnant. Seven years together had not netted a commitment from my boyfriend, and we were unable to come to mutual agreement that would allow the relationship to grow and prosper. Although I couldn't see it at the time, he actually did me a favor by leaving the relationship.

"Basically," she added, "I was in a dead-end career, dead-end relationship, and dead-end life. What I initially perceived as catastrophic change ended up being the best thing that could have ever happened to me. Although these changes were brutal and heart-wrenching at the time, ultimately they resulted in choices that produced a better quality of life, a job with greater personal satisfaction and a committed, fulfilling new relationship."

In her quest for self-healing, Carol studied alternative approaches to healing such as herbology and acupressure. She decided she'd like to share with others the healing techniques she had learned, and acquired a professional massage therapist license. In just a few short years, she's built up a steady practice and now sets her own hours, which allows time for the leisure and social activities of her choice. Her hourly fee is double what she made in sales, and she's gradually acquiring financial stability. Although it will take some years to rebuild her credit history, she was given a small mortgage-free condominium that is virtually maintenance-free by a deceased relative.

Furthermore, she met a new love while training to become a massage therapist. "Karl's a masseuse, too," Carol says enthusiastically. "We share many common interests and goals, and in our spare time, there's lots of *hands-on* practice of new massage techniques on each other," she says with a Mona Lisa like smile. Although they have not set a definite date, they have discussed marriage, and Carol feels a great deal of relief at Karl's lack of commitment-phobia.

When asked what she has learned from the experience, Carol pauses for a moment of reflection and then responds softly, "Just this. The natural order of life is change. Nothing is static. From moment to moment, everything is in a perpetual state of change. If we resist change, we deny ourselves the opportunity for growth. We have the greatest potential for change at midlife because it's the midpoint of life experience." She takes a deep breath and continues, "It's like riding a see-saw. There's no way you can maintain equilibrium indefinitely. At some point, you're going to either rise into the air or fall to the ground. It's just the natural order of change or movement. The trick is not to panic if the seesaw goes crashing to the ground. Just put your feet down," she says with a gentle laugh, "and push yourself back up into the air."

The majority of women do not experience the degree of change that Carol experienced. In fact, many women find themselves in the opposite position experiencing little or no change in midlife years. This, in turn, may result in non-growth and portend an impending crisis.

Jenny is 52 years old, a homemaker who has been married for 30 years and menopausal for the past five. "I had the typical symptoms," she confides, "hot flashes, mood swings, erratic menstrual periods, weight gain and a lack of sex drive. My body was undergoing change but my life was not. On the surface, everything seemed ideal. I had a beautiful home, financial security, no serious health problems and a faithful husband who held a prestigious position in the community.

"On the outside, everything seemed great, but on the inside," she admits, "I was very unhappy. My husband and I had grown apart, the children had left home, and I had no real hobbies or interests other than an occasional game of bridge or golf. I was often left alone for long hours due to my husband's career and became increasingly angry at and resentful of his physical and emotional distance. I didn't see divorce as a viable option and couldn't find a way out of the quagmire I was in.

"I was so afraid of change", she continues, "that I would rather stay in an unhappy but known environment rather than risk the unknown potential for change. The longer I refused to consider any sort of change in my routine, the more miserable I became. Worse yet, I blamed my husband for my unhappiness," she explains, "rather than recognize that I was the one who had to change in order to bring my life back into balance."

Jenny contacted her regular physician for menopausal treatment options. Fortunately, he recognized her problem wasn't solely physical. In addition to placing her on hormonal medication to regulate her body, he referred her to a counselor to help her understand the body-mind connection. "What my therapist helped me realize," Jenny explains, "is that unless I faced change head-on, there was little chance for me to move out of my *stuck state* and lead a happy, productive life. No one was going to wave a magic wand and make all my problems go away," she said. "I had to take responsibility.

"My therapist had me examine various areas of my life such as relationship, career, leisure, finance, health and education to determine my level of satisfaction in each. If there was dissatisfaction in any area, we discussed possible options for change, settled upon the most viable option, and then conscientiously acted on it," she said. "For example, I sincerely believed the bulk of my unhappiness stemmed from my husband spending so many hours on the job. However, when I looked deeper into my feelings," she acknowledged, "I was surprised to discover that I was really more unhappy with myself than with him." Jenny adds, "In fact, I was proud of the work he did and the respect he had earned from the community, and, as much as I wanted him to spend more time with me, I really didn't want him to quit his job to do it.

What I really felt," she confides, "Was that I was only recognized through his achievements and not through my own. Subsequently, my therapist suggested I consider possible career options," she states. "Since we didn't really need the money and I wasn't specialized in any particular field, I decided to volunteer my time to a well-known charitable organization. I feel really good about the time I'm devoting to a worthy cause and the recognition I receive from family, friends and the press. I'm no longer viewed solely as an extension of my husband. I've achieved a certain amount of respect and recognition on my own.

"Furthermore," she adds, "my husband and I enjoy sitting down together in the evening and sharing news of what's taken place in our jobs. He doesn't avoid me now that I'm not angry and resentful, and we spend more time together. It's a win-win situation," she says with a big smile, "not only for me and my husband, but for the community, as well."

In addition to embarking upon a new career, Jenny also decided to further her education and recently began a course in computer training. The campus is not far from her home, and she and a friend bicycle to class twice a week. With the exercise, hormonal medication and new outlook on life, she's dropped 12 pounds, and friends tell her she has never looked better. To sum up, Jenny says, "Our bodies are great teachers. In retrospect I can now see that the physical changes happening in my body were a subtle sign that changes needed to happen in my environment, as well. By facing change head-on, my life has radically transformed in a positive new direction. I've never been happier."

Although all women naturally undergo menopausal change during midlife, some are able to pass through it more effortlessly than others. In fact, rather than a time of turmoil and angst, many women consider midlife the most fulfilling time of their lives. Social psychologist Orville Gilbert Brim, Director of the MacArthur Foundation Research Network on Successful Midlife Development and president of Life Trends Inc. reports, "The surprising thing is that midlife may be the best time, the best place to be." His comments reflect the findings of a groundbreaking 10-year study conducted on 7,800 Americans (3,000 between the ages of 35 and 65) who answered more than 1,100 questions. "People give midlife a very high satisfaction rating. That surprised all of us," Brim said.

In my own work as a ministerial counselor over the past two decades with a predominantly female clientele, there has been one undeniable determining factor between the fundamentally happy midlife woman and the one who has difficulty adapting to the change. Change is the very essence of our being. Every day, we slough off dead skin cells that are replaced with new skin cells. Within one year's time, we are totally new beings, cellularly.

Change affords us the opportunity to expand and evolve, to move beyond limitation and entropy. To embrace change is to embrace growth, and it is in our growth that we become actualized human beings.

> *There is no better exercise for the heart than reaching down and lifting someone else up.*

Metamorphosis

Pat Drewry

Pat is a private psychotherapist, psychiatric nurse and Healing Touch Practitioner. She is an advisor and lecturer and also runs a therapeutic arts program for at-risk children. Pat can be contacted at pdrewry@sisna.com.

I look back at my own midlife struggles from the vantage of 58 years of living—and from the perspective of a psychotherapist for twenty of those years. What I see is that most of the women I know faced dramatic shifts in values in the second half of their lives. Unless they bury their heads in the sand, they undergo a great deal of turmoil in their lives, but after the turmoil they emerge as happier, healthier people with a greater sense of personal power.

My experience of these transitions has been full of exciting, evolutionary changes—mixed with loss, pain and loneliness. Despite the discomfort of occasionally facing what I would rather avoid, I still seek greater consciousness, and I experience life fully and passionately. I am convinced that no one can progress toward one's potential without overcoming sometimes soul-wrenching challenges. Another part of my experience is that the more I move through this evolutionary process, the more I become conscious of my—and all of our—interconnectedness with the universe. Thus there is a paradox: as we each become more complete as individuals we also become more aware of being part of a greater whole.

Buddhists emphasize that the quality of journey is at least as important as the value of the destination. Embracing this philosophy has taught me to respond to the potential of new insights with a more relaxed and open mind. The discipline of daily meditation has enabled me to peacefully stop, look and listen to life instead of rushing resolutely forward with some pre-programmed agenda.

Fellow seekers are also important. The sharing and support of friends and community creates an atmosphere of belonging that benefits each person's health.

My story really begins with my family. My grandmother had little outlet for her midlife power. I wondered what I would have been like in the early 1900's had I been the bright Wellesley College-educated woman that she was. Her leadership skills were constrained to the few avenues available to her—the social and literary clubs at the university where my grandfather was a professor. As far back as I can remember, the men in my family roundly criticized her for usurping power as a *general* or *boss*. They suggested her domination caused my mother's psychotic breakdown when I was five. As a child, I quickly learned that women with strong wills were not desirable.

Like most women of my generation, my first career was marrying and raising a family, I married the man I had loved since high school. We held on to each other through college and were married two days after he graduated. (I had finished the year before and worked nearby so we could see each other often.) During the presidency of John Kennedy, I had dreams of going into the Peace Corps, but I could not imagine telling him or my family that I was going to do anything other than follow through with our plans for marriage. We were both inexperienced with relationships, so we found comfort and security with each other.

Our early life was something of a bumpy road. He was a military pilot and served three tours of duty during the Vietnam War. I was deeply affected by the many months of forced separation, which demanded developing independence and acting on my own in spite of the loneliness. By the time we reached our 40s and our children were maturing, we were forced to confront the differences in our values and priorities.

When we were both 41, I returned to school for a Master's Degree as an advanced practice psychiatric nurse. In the meantime, he was becoming very successful in the business world. Our three children were approaching or in adolescence and developing their own independence, which they were verbalizing or acting-out—not always to our liking. My counseling skills helped me listen to and understand their perspectives, but their father found it more difficult. His skills in management and sales only reinforced his unwavering perspective, and we began to disagree more openly as our career biases supported our sharply different approaches to life and relationships.

On the job, I was being driven to assert myself as a leader. This new stirring occurred about a year after I began my first full time job—a trainer at a mental health agency in charge of developing a network of volunteer parent educators from the community. I was now a *professional*, not merely someone's wife or mother. I learned more effective ways of parenting and I also began to express my opinions more openly and effectively with my husband and other adults.

As a result, our marriage began to slowly unravel. I remember often creeping into my private study in the middle of a sleepless night and writing reams of pages after a bitter or confusing argument between us. Contrary to all recommendations for happy marriages, we usually had our more difficult conversations at bedtime because it was the only alone time we had without the children. I felt sad and guilty as I emptied my hurt and confused feelings about my husband on paper. Then I would carefully hide my book away so that he would never encounter my uncertainties and experience hurt from my words.

One of my promises to myself since the age of ten was to avoid debilitating mental illness in myself or my family. Feeling the need for professional help, I began a series of sessions with a therapist. With her guidance I began to see more effective ways of coping. I gradually became clearer about my identity and felt a freedom of expression I had never had before.

As a result of my changing there were bright moments as my husband and I gained new insights in our relationship. I was becoming more balanced—and not overreacting to life's situations.

Just before my 50th birthday, I was invited to join a group of psychiatric nurses visiting The People's Republic of China. The purpose of our tour was to provide for interchange between psychiatric clinicians from the two countries. I had never gone on a trip without my family, however the impulse to be a part of this trip was too strong to resist. It turned out that this would be a pivotal event in my life. Despite the oppressive communist political regime, I was struck by the sensitivity and intelligence of the Chinese people, as well as by their hunger to talk about spiritual matters. My mind and spirit seemed to open on an unconscious level to prepare me for the many changes that were about to occur.

As soon as I returned, I learned that our oldest son, who suffered from depressive episodes and anxiety, had decided to drop out of college in his junior year until he knew "what I really want to do." I could only hope that he would see a therapist instead of self-medicating with marijuana. Through many restless nights I worried about him and associated my fears of mental illness with my concerns for his future. I was a parent educator and therapist by then, yet I could not help my own child. My frustration was exacerbated by the fact that my husband and I held completely divergent views regarding our son's needs.

On the other hand, my strong psychological need to avoid the experience of *brokenness* that I associated with my defective childhood family drove me to ignore aspects of myself that did not fit the acceptable image of the perfect woman my husband expected—or that I thought he expected.

In 1991, my increasing sense of isolation intensified as we watched the nightmare of the Gulf War on television. My husband was experiencing flashbacks from his Vietnam experiences, but he could not draw himself away from the replay of each day's air war. Finally he decided to see a therapist. I began to feel hope that we could find a way to be more emotionally and intimately present for each other. I had begun to realize that my determination to keep our marriage together may not be healthy for either of us, but I was afraid of the impact of divorce on our children and me.

Two months after he began therapy, my husband decided he wanted a separation. When he told me, I felt shock and fear, but there was also something like a cool, refreshing breeze going throughout my body. He was excited about moving into his own place and selecting his new apartment and furnishings. I felt a complex sense of loss and empathy for the excitement and new energy that I had not seen in him in a long time. When I was not simply numb, I was feeling guilt over a sense of being freed up and hurt that my husband would choose to leave me.

Ultimately, our marriage ended at the 30-year mark when we were both 52.

After our daughter, our youngest child, had graduated from high school, she and I moved to a condo. I went to dinner and the theater with single friends and became a much more involved member of my church. I did not have a desire to date, although my fantasies included a new partner. I knew I was not ready to become involved in another long-term relationship, but I was afraid of the hurt of rejection and loss that would probably come with more temporary ones. I saw myself as a butterfly in a cocoon, and my job was to evolve into the whole being I was intended to be.

My daughter left for college about two months after we moved. Her confusion and hurt about our divorce as well as several traumatic personal violations left her unprepared to begin a new life. She was extremely sensitive and highly artistic which seemed to make her susceptible to the cruelties of life's passages. As a result, she was unable to adjust to college life and abruptly left after two months in a distant State. From there, she began her own journey into a mystical underworld accompanied by a broken but sensitive man.

In a telephone call, she told me with great excitement that she was leaving school and going off with the man of her dreams whom she had met four days before. Nothing I said could deter her. I sat in the dark at 2 a.m. trembling with a gut wrenching sense of panic. I was terrified about her mental health and safety, but this 18-year-old "adult" was thousands of miles away, and I was totally helpless

I had nowhere to turn but God. My three years of daily meditation were preparatory for that moment, and, as a result, I was able to experience a warmth of spirit that confirmed that I was not alone.

The next five years were punctuated with times of hope and reconciliation between us and periods of not knowing where or how she was. I knew that I was deepening and expanding in ways I had never imagined was possible, so I believed there had to be a divine purpose to all this that was beyond human understanding.

My mother had a stroke a few months after my daughter abandoned college, and, since I was the only one of three children in the same city with her, by default, I became the manager of her care. She recovered partially but had broken her hip and required someone to be home with her all the time. I found myself overseeing her care and managing her finances.

For three months during my mother's illness, my daughter and her partner came home to help. For a while that was comforting, but my daughter's partner began to drink, and I had to ask him to leave. She left with him.

Mother died a year after her first stroke. That year, 1995, was a significant one for me. I was able to overcome the fears that my mother had imbued into me. She was always terrified that one of us would get "sick" and end up in the psychiatric ward as she had. Even as a ten-year-old child, I was aware of the differences between her and others. Being an artist and poet, she enjoyed being unique— "original" she called it. I decided I wanted to be as *normal* as possible and not do anything that would stand out as being *different*. After she died it seemed I was set free from those restrictions.

A dramatic change in my consciousness came with my introduction to Healing Touch Therapy. Healing Touch is a program that facilitates self-healing by balancing and clearing the energy field. I had been very skeptical in the past, but I was becoming far more open since my experiences in China. After some initial training, I became a believer, however I was still afraid of being different, so I did not know if and when I would incorporate it in my practice. When a desperate client came to me, closed to all the usual talk-therapy interventions, I offered to do *something different*. She called the next morning to tell me she had her first experience of inner peace ever.

A year after the first class, I started training in earnest to become a Healing Touch therapist and began to combine my talk therapy with Healing Touch. Gradually, I relaxed, and my fear of being different began to evaporate.

Another important influence in my midlife journey was my increasing awareness of my body. I had never been very conscious of the feelings and senses in my body until I began meditation. Before that, I saw my body as a sexual object—about which I was uncomfortable—and as something very uncoordinated. Dance helped me gain more grace and coordination. This process of awakening to my body has continued as I added the practice of yoga in the last year. The important thing for me was to explore different techniques and to be open to change. By letting go of old, restricted beliefs I freed myself to be all I was meant to be. That is what is important.

Before I set off to a new life in a distant city, many friends gathered to give me a wonderful party and to celebrate our friendship and love. I felt as if my dream had come true and I was bursting out of the cocoon with joyous laughter. My fears of rejection for being different, unique or eccentric were dissolved as I experienced deeper, more heartfelt relationships than I ever had before. I truly became my metamorphosed self. I am now the butterfly spreading my wings and flying.

When you help someone up a mountain, you'll find yourself close to the summit, too.

CHAPTER NINE

COMMUNICATION BEYOND WORDS

The previous chapters have talked about the sometimes-dramatic philosophical and spiritual changes that accompany the midlife transition. Sometimes normal language fails us as we attempt to explain these changes both to ourselves and to others close to us. This chapter deals with approaches and techniques that go beyond the normal way of looking at life. They can be a great source of inspiration and comfort.

ART AS AN INSPIRATIONAL TOOL

Jacqueline Ripstein

Jacqueline Ripstein is an internationally renowned artist. She holds a patent for discovering a new technique in art (invisible art and light technique which makes the invisible world become visible). Her legacy is to bring art to a new dimension for guidance and healing. She has been included as an extraordinary talent by the U.S. government and has been awarded the titles of the Most Admired Woman of the Decade and one of 2,000 Outstanding People of the 20th Century. She has been commissioned by the Holy Family Institute to paint "Our Lady of the Universe" which is now touring the U.S. Jacqueline can be contacted at JRipstein8@aol.com

Many of us live in a world of overwhelming, non-fulfilling stress. The journey we choose may be a route that is familiar but not leading us where we want to go.

A new road beckons when we realize that the old road is not working. The choice to change directions in our hands—but it is one that consumes a lot of energy as we are generally not comfortable with change.

Indeed, some limitations are self-imposed. Besides this, our physical senses are very limited. We think that what we perceive with them is the only reality, but our view is so narrow. As with the iceberg, we see the tip, thinking that that is all, but the majority of it is unseen and unknown.

We may experience a physical, emotional or spiritual message that our soul recognizes. We may hear a voice inside us reconfirming our search and guiding us to transformation. We may see that *light of the moment* that awakens us. Each of these is the spark of Art. The fire this spark kindles inspires us to take the steps necessary for our own development—and to take them with faith and conviction.

As you take this path, prepare to claim your inner power with the trust that life has a perfect order that transcends your understanding of it. Recognize that all that happens is for your own benefit—even though at the moment, you may not able to see the lesson. If you accept this, you will then be ready to see the world differently. This will allow you to find the various gifts that were given to you—and that you have never opened. One of them is your creativity.

Creativity connects directly to your energy, to your soul. When you make the connection, you plug into the infinite. As a result, when we create we open our lives to infinite possibilities. Art in its diverse manifestations is one of them. Art can be a direct connection with your soul—one of your tools to regain the connection within yourself.

While we are all in touch with art in some way, we each have a different approach to it. In fact, it does not matter if you create art or merely observe it; the process will take you along the path. And where does the path lead?

Our society hungers for peace and love. Our failure to deliver this essential diet has created a spiritual malnutrition in our children. Looking at our youth, we can see they are suffering more than ever. They have also lost the connection to the creativity within themselves. Following the path of creativity will transform them and help awaken all of us from modern society's "sleeping chaos". It is time to stimulate the hearts, spirits and minds of people worldwide to touch their creativity, to come to the safe harbor of transcendent values across a sea of raging materialism

For my journey of the path, many times I have painted various Biblical scenes as a starting point. For me, these provide a fountain of inspiration that generates ideas, emotions and learning. Sometimes images of the past and symbols that our subconscious mind can decode have the power to activate our conscious mind. When these unconscious codes are recalled, they give us an opportunity for healing, nurturing and evoking feelings within ourselves that have been covered by many layers of emotional and spiritual insulation. To be an artist is to be in connection with the creation of life.

Art has many venues of expression—Painting, Sculpture, Literature, Music, Dance, etc. Each has many things in common with the others. One of those things is that they are each pure expression of the soul. Another is that they each resonate with nature and the vibrations of the universe

Transformation through art takes place when you are sufficiently inspired by it to take the steps necessary to understand your spiritual growth process. To do that, you must let go of the past and receive the present as a gift. As we grow, the world we are living in will grow as well.

We each have artistic and creative abilities. It is one of our natural ways of expressing our inner feelings. You can use this ability without even recognizing it in your everyday living. By applying creativity to your daily life, that life becomes exciting and receptive to inspiration. Even cooking can be creative and artistic. Each time you try something different, you open the boundaries of your mind a little more than before. Then the universe helps you discover new choices for living your life in a more authentic way—opening yourself to the possibility of making your life a piece of art. Art is a prayer that, done with gratitude, brings order, harmony, joy and beauty to all our lives.

Art is a communication. Whether you are creating art or you are being what I call the *observer artist*, you are connected to the moment of the creation. What I call *to be an Artist* is not merely about being the one who performs. It is also about being those who approach a piece of art with openness and sensitivity. How can a piece of art be complete if it is only performed? Emptiness would come if it were one sided, if it were unshared.

The universe uses an artist as an instrument, creating a finite moment from of infinite inspiration. Every heart that is in touch with that moment feels that, in some sense, time is meaningless, because art transcends it. A very powerful piece of art transmits vibrations that influence our energy, charging us with spiritual light. When you first connect with a work of art, these vibrations will inspire you, creating a feeling that may last for days. Later, as you recall that moment of first contact, the same feeling of inspiration can return, fresh and pure.

Carl Jung said, "Spirit lies behind the collective unconscious, and art reveals the unconscious." An artist taps into the fountain of creation to make visible what has already been created. As artists, we must consider each day as a blank canvas, as a challenge to touch spirit and create. Each day has its purpose—a purpose for each of us to learn and from which to grow. Art unites humanity. It is truly a universal language that has no boundaries.

We are living in a time that is ready for the recognition of our gifts and our inner power. It is our time to free ourselves from the past by being creative in life and jointly co-creating a new piece of art. This piece of art is a New World, thanking and honoring Mother Earth for embracing us in her womb, for allowing us the great opportunity of our awakening. A new day is dawning; sunrise is here; we are now claiming our gifts. The choice is yours to use your powers, your tools and your artistry to create the life you deserve—a life of joy, love peace and light.

Communication Beyond Words

Inside you there's an Artist you don't know about.
Say "yes" quickly, if you know, if you've known it
from before the beginning of the universe.

— Jalai Ud-Din Rumi

Photography as a Universal Communicator

Béla Kalman

In 1984, Béla Kalman was given a lifetime appointment as Master of the International Federation of Artistic Photographers, a title held by only 25 photographers. He is the only one appointed from the United States. Béla has won 17 medals and has had nineteen one-man shows. His work is included in the permanent collections of eighteen museums. When I asked Béla what his philosophy is, he replied, "Dare to do things. I want to be remembered as the man who reached for the stars." One of Béla's photographs graces the cover of this book. He can be reached at (617) 236-0040.

In 1839, Louis Jacques Mandé Daguerre patented the camera in Paris, France. Twenty years later photographs were as common as the cell phones are today. Today, photography is an art form, a worldwide tool for the press and the basis of the most dynamic forms of telecommunication, truly confirming the notion that a picture is worth a thousand words. No verbal language is necessary to communicate meaning by photography (although sometimes captions explain or give context.) This revolutionary invention now, 160 years later, speaks directly to six billion people.

Image making has gone far beyond the *camera obscura* as it was originally conceived. Some of the most memorable photographic images bring us closer to the feel of history. We now can see how tall Abe Lincoln was or how wet it was during D-Day. Today, photographic-based imagery has gone far beyond recreating images our eyes could have captured. Now, all medical fields use the fruits of photography, from x-rays to heat generated images.

Visual communication now takes just seconds. It connects the farthest reaches of the world with centers of culture and commerce, shrinking our universe and creating Marshall McLuhan's global village. Telecommunication takes us where no one has gone before, giving us images of the far side of the Moon and close ups of Mars. Dozens of satellites provide photographic images to predict weather patterns and monitor our world.

Originally a tool for documentation, photography quickly became art form as well. This tool for painting with light has dramatically changed our perspectives on common subjects with its unique images. Some photographs repeat and overlay images for effect and use all the colors of the spectrum. Some underwater photography elicits colors and shapes that can only be created with special camera lenses and lighting. Other photos create perspectives from a bird's eye view or a groundhog's.

The field of photography is constantly in flux. Today, photographs are used as memorabilia, entertainment, information, sales tools, political statements, mood changers, serious art and pathways to heightened awareness. I have spent sixty years doing photography, and I am delighted to see that it is something everyone can participate in. Cameras range from disposable toys to lifetime companions, from inexpensive tools to major investments, from completely automatic to fully manual. There is an affordable price range and technical complexity for everyone.

I use the camera to stimulate people's imagination, show beauty in various ways and present different perspectives to reach into one's soul. Through my photographs, I act to connect the observer with an aspect of the world as I see it.

Most of us have used photographs to document people or events, but the camera has additional value as you approach changes in the very essence of your life. Looking at the world through the lens of a camera changes your perspective by forcing you to stop the phenomena of a world in constant flux and focus on a discrete moment in time. The experience of the world as all one piece expands as you begin to see the interconnected elements one at a time.

How might you use photography to help you see the world and your place in it differently? Here are some suggestions. If you are just starting, an automatic focusing camera might be best. Explore your surroundings through the viewfinder. Look at your dwelling, your room and objects in your environment that are important to you. When you see something you like, photograph it. Use natural light rather than flash. Fujicolor 800 ASA is a very good film for photographing in low light without having to use flash.

After you have explored your surroundings, explore how you see other people. Again, explore them through your viewfinder. Do not pose or direct them, but let them be natural, doing what they do. When you think you see their essence, take a photograph. Do the same thing with nature, looking for both big and small things of beauty and meaning.

If you feel adventurous, and if your camera has a self timer, try taking self portraits. In these you will be posing yourself as you want to be seen by your self or by others.

As a final exercise, use your camera to expand your consciousness. Look through your viewfinder to see meaning in the interplay of light and dark. In this exercise, you are not looking for things to photograph, but essence. When you see something inspiring, press the shutter.

It is the seeing through the camera that first changes your focus. Looking at the resulting photographs reminds you of your shifted focus and allows you to remember the experience. Both the process (photographing) and the products (photographs) can cause you to see the world and your place in it in an entirely new way.

HARNESSING THE HEALING POWERS OF SOUND

Steven Halpern

Steven Halpern is a composer, recording artist and sound healer who has released over 50 albums. Steven has received international recognition for his pioneering work promoting the use of music for healing, meditation and inner peace. His music has been heard on CBS's 48 Hours and John Bradshaw's PBS series. He is the author of the forthcoming book Sound Healing in the New Millennium. *For a free catalogue, call (800) 909-0707 or visit Steven at* http://www.stevenhalpern.com.

Music and your moods

Recently, there has been an explosion of interest in choosing and using music to improve our lives. Best-selling books and numerous articles in mainstream women's magazines appear like spring flowers. However, many of the authors do not truly understand their subject matter. Another source of confusion is the very preliminary research that focused on Mozart's music as the panacea for just about anything. I would like to clarify the role of sound so that you can set your life to music in a much more effective manner than ever before.

The relationship between music and mood is many faceted. There are some aspects that are universal—and some that are very individual. That is why it is of paramount importance that you monitor your own responses carefully. Don't take anyone else's word as the final authority (even mine). Ultimately, you must trust yourself, but first you'll need to become more aware of your own responses so that you can take responsibility for making appropriate choices.

Let me suggest a brief overview that will help you understand how you respond to sound vibrations. This brief section will sharpen your awareness more effectively and more practically than most semester-long music classes.

1. Your body is a self-healing instrument—if you give it a chance. Your body is genetically programmed to heal itself. I would suggest that sound-healing assists the body to come into its natural state of balance and harmony.
2. Although there are many paths to nurturing your body, mind and spirit, the common denominator of the vast majority of approaches emphasizes that you are most effective in a state of *deep relaxation*.
3. Using music to evoke the *relaxation response* is one of the simplest and most effective ways of all—but you MUST choose the right music. Most music was *not* composed for this purpose.

Although we are all individuals, we also all share certain vibrational and structural common denominators. With respect to the ways that we respond to sound, two concepts are key. They are universal, and are not contingent on your personal taste or favorite style of music.

Rhythm entrainment

The most basic factor that determines how we respond to music is *the beat*. One of the most powerful effects that music has on our nervous system is called *rhythm entrainment*. This refers to the physical phenomenon whereby an external rhythmic stimulus, such as the drum or basic pulse in a musical composition, involuntarily causes the listener's heartbeat to match its speed. This means that a *fast rhythm* inevitably produces *a fast heartbeat*—the complete antithesis of relaxation. For many people, trying to relax while listening to fast music is like driving a car with your foot on the brake and the gas pedal at the same time.

Anticipation response

The second factor relates to our mental response. We have been culturally conditioned to follow melodic, harmonic and rhythmic patterns in music. Whenever we listen to traditional classical or pop selections, we are unconsciously hooked into following the structure—and projecting that structure into the future. In my workshops, I demonstrate this *paralysis of analysis* by singing the first seven notes of a scale: "do-re-mi-fa-so-la-ti..." and I do not finish the final "do". It is always a delight to watch people holding their breath, or actually singing the note out loud for completion. It was just too stressful for them to leave the pattern of notes uncompleted. This approach to tension and resolution is the basic for most Western classical compositions. That is precisely *why* most selections are generally unsuitable or inappropriate as a choice for evoking relaxation.

Setting your sacred space with sacred sound

There is a long and honored place in most spiritual traditions for sacred sound. Church bells, Tibetan meditation gongs and 'singing bowls', as well as Gregorian or Vedic (Hindu) chant, are just some of the examples. David soothed King Saul with his harp.

What music do you choose to soothe your soul? Until 1975, that was a fairly moot question. There weren't any albums specifically composed for meditation and inner work, and the few recorded albums of chant were typically hard to find items even in specialized record stores. That all began to change with the release of *Spectrum Suite*. The notes on the album jacket openly stated that the intent of this music was to relax the body and soothe the soul.

Twenty-five years later, there are many albums to choose from. Entire sections in Borders, BestBuy and Barnes and Noble—as well as independent book and music retailers—now attest to a growing audience for soul-soothing music and the music industry's willingness to meet it with a veritable flood of releases. As with any trend in which the *bandwagon effect* operates, the consumer has to learn to separate the wheat from the chaff.

The importance of assembling your own library of nurturing sounds is reinforced by no less an icon than Oprah. Her segments on *Remembering the Spirit* have awakened millions to the spiritual dimension of their lives. Clearly, there is something more to life than many were lead to believe by their parents or religious training.

One of the best ways to know *the real you* is to listen to the *still, small voice* inside. This suggestion is found in many spiritual traditions. As many have discovered, one listens best in silence. However, many people are so used to constant sound in their lives that they are initially uncomfortable if there is no music, TV or other background sound to fill the void. This is all the more proof that, to find their still, small voice, people really need to create an *oasis of silence*, a private retreat, if only to visit for a few moments.

A sound approach to silence

When you recognize this truth, you can employ time-honored techniques to use especially composed music to lead you into *the silence*. Indeed, some of this music becomes so transparent that you can even let it continue playing during your silent moments.

When you choose the right music, you can turn off the mental and emotional responses that accompany most music. Here's more good news. Even if you have never studied music in your life, it's never too late to appreciate music in this way.

Listening to music as a doorway to the ineffable is easy. The key is to choose the right music. For some, Gregorian chant may work. One of the recordings that has a proven track record, and which has a built-in capacity to evoke the relaxation response, is *Spectrum Suite*. Another good choice would be *Gifts of the Angels*.

The listening technique I've taught for more than 25 years is deceptively simple. The key is to give yourself the uninterrupted time and space to do it. Remember, you deserve it. If you have a decent set of headphones, put them on. Take a deep breath. Close your eyes—and as the music begins, allow the music to carry you into space between the notes—into the space where you *become* the music.

Even if it's only for five minutes at first, you'll be able to feel the difference. You may become aware of a melting of tension in your neck and shoulders. You'll probably notice that you are breathing more deeply and slowly than before. This is a good thing. Subtle changes occur in your body chemistry when the relaxation response is evoked. Your mood is uplifted due to the release of endorphins, a special class of neurotransmitters.

It seems that we are genetically programmed to feel good when we treat ourselves this way. What a wonderful bit of positive reinforcement directly from our biology! The process works automatically—if you just give it a chance. Deep relaxation and meditation give it that chance.

Start with five minutes at a time. Create periods in your daily schedule when you can enter your *sacred space*—when you can sit in your special corner or in your room or under a tree or by a lake—and *tune in*.

Music for goal setting and reflection

In my workshops, I have met a consistently large percentage of individuals who felt that something was the matter with them because they didn't get the same amazing results that were promised in best-selling books like *Superlearning* and *The Mozart Effect*. I believe I know the reason why.

Some people are pre-wired to respond to certain forms of music—like that of Mozart—in a way that helps them focus and concentrate; others find that such classically-structured music actually *distracts them* and makes it harder to concentrate or to be creative.

To help you hear that still, silent voice, *you want music that allows you to focus on yourself—rather than music that draws attention to itself*. Unfortunately, most music is designed to be so interesting that our minds are unconsciously *hooked* into following the melody, harmony or lyrics or emotional content. That is one of the motivating factors underpinning every title in my Inner Peace Music® series.

Writing your own script

Another functional use of music is to serve as the background for *your own self-scripted affirmations*. Many people are familiar with using these short, positive statements to help them achieve a goal or change certain behavior. Some people write them down on a piece of paper and paste them on a mirror, the refrigerator or a wall. If you take time to allow your mind to become quiet, sometimes ideas and goals for your personal or spiritual improvement will just pop into mind.

If you're having a problem coming up with a script for your own affirmations or goals, try playing *Enhancing Creativity* in the background. This can help get your creative juices flowing while you're at your computer, sitting with a pad of paper, or just dreaming. You might also play this program as you drift into sleep. Set your intention, and trust that the answers will come. Sometimes they come while the music is playing, sometimes at other moments. The important thing is that the process is in motion.

You might also consider writing a simple affirmation to yourself, for example, "The most appropriate goals for me now come to me in thoughts or dreams." Consider speaking them into a tape recorder, with a variety of music as background. Most people find that when they are in a deeply relaxed state, the self-talk sinks in deeper.

Harnessing the power of your subconscious mind

According to the most current research, *harnessing the power of your subconscious mind* is one of the best ways to help create the life experience you want. Many leaders in the field—such as Deepak Chopra, Louise Hay, and Brian Tracy—recommend incorporating affirmations (short, positive suggestions) into your program for personal and professional growth. One of the most effective ways of working with affirmations is to listen to them.

The science of *subliminal* (below the threshold of conscious awareness) communication offers a powerful modality for change. Even though you do not actually *hear* the affirmations, your subconscious mind *does perceive* them—and responds accordingly. The most effective way to access your subconscious mind and increase your receptivity is to listen in a state of deep relaxation, that is, when you are in the *alpha* or *theta* brainwave zone. Clinically tested and proven music, such as the recordings that comprise the *Inner Peace* series and the *SoundWave 2000*™ series, effectively anchor you in that state. This virtually guarantees that you receive the maximum benefit.

The unique nature of this music *decreases stress* and *fine-tunes the mind* into the frequencies of *alpha* and *theta* brainwave activity. These states are associated with heightened creativity. Unlike most music, compositions that effectively do this often become *transparent* and seem to disappear as they play softly in the background. Their ambient nature and gentle flow promote a relaxed yet alert state that listeners report actually increases with continued use.

Creativity, relaxation and flow

For thousands of years, people have sought to invoke the muse of creativity. A key factor in many approaches involves getting yourself into a deeply relaxed state. In a state of deep relaxation, we attune to "the field of infinite possibilities" as Deepak Chopra puts it. No matter what you call it—connecting with God, universal truth, Higher Power, Higher Self, the zone of creativity—the key is to allow the energy to flow through you. Although we do not fully understand the mechanisms by which it occurs, creativity flows more easily when we allow our body and mind to become quiet and peaceful. In a sense, this is a functional benefit of the universal, spiritual psycho-technology that states: "Be still and know."

Ancient sages and contemporary experts emphasize the importance of creating *an inner oasis of serenity* and recommend spending at least twenty minutes a day in this state. Give yourself periods of silent contemplation to quiet the endless chatter of the mind and allow the still, small voice to be heard. There are many ways to do this: deep breathing, meditation, Zen walking, running, yoga—or listening to certain music. The right recording can help you access a deeply relaxed state of being and supercharge your creativity—at work or home.

A sound approach to happiness

Listening to music for pleasure is something we do almost instinctively. When we listen to music we enjoy, a certain class of neuropeptides and neurotransmitters known as endorphins are released in our bodies. These chemicals are associated with feelings of happiness and well-being, and enhancement of the immune system. We generate them ourselves, so—best of all—they are free, legal and non-fattening!

I recommend listening to your favorite music, at least some of the time, with headphones. They can deliver high-quality sound in a very effective manner, without disturbing anyone else. Closing your eyes as well allows you to block out the visual distractions that keep you anchored in the ordinary environment, and away from contact with your inner, higher self. Even if it's only for five minutes, make those *your* five minutes. This is what Shirley MacLaine was so articulate in expressing in her landmark book, *Going Within*.

So set aside some time to listen—just for you!

Chapter Ten

Mid-Laugh Opportunity

This chapter is about using humor to change your perspective of the world and to reduce stress and gain insight in the process. It is appropriate that we begin with a story.

One day three men are out having a relaxing day fishing, when suddenly they catch a mermaid. After hauling the mermaid up in a net, she promises that if the men set her free, in return she will grant each of them a wish.

The first man doesn't believe it so he says, "Alright, if you can really grant wishes, then double my IQ." The mermaid says, "Done," and suddenly, the first man starts to flawlessly recite Shakespeare and analyze it with extreme insight.

The second man is so amazed, he looks at the mermaid and says, "Triple my IQ." The mermaid says, "Done," and the second man starts to recite solutions to all of the mathematical problems that have been stumping all of the scientists in various fields from physics to chemistry.

The third man is so enthralled with the changes in his friends, he says to the mermaid, "Quintuple my IQ." The mermaid looks at him and says, "You know, I normally don't try to change people's minds when they make a wish, but I really wish you'd reconsider." The man responds, "Nope, I want you to increase my IQ times five, and if you don't do it, I won't set you free."

"Please," said the mermaid "You don't know what you're asking. It'll change your entire view on the universe. Won't you ask for something else...a million dollars, anything?"

But no matter what the mermaid said, the third man insisted on having his IQ increased to five times its power. So the mermaid finally relented and said, "Done."

The third man became a woman.

Using Humor to Design the Future

Steve Bhaerman

Steve is a writer and comedian who has written and performed for the past twelve years as "Swami Beyondananda." As the Swami, he has written three books, including his latest Duck Soup for the Soul, *a celebration of the healing power of humor written in Swami's own inimitable style. Steve also travels around the country—and the world—offering his workshop on the Alchemy of Humor. He can be reached at* swamib@saber.net.

Laughter heals. It's been said so often it's almost a cliché. There's the now-famous story of how writer Norman Cousins, faced with a life-threatening illness, holed himself up in a hotel room with Marx Brothers movies and Candid Camera re-runs—and made a remarkable recovery. Since that time over thirty-five years ago, scientists have made more detailed studies of the physiological benefits of laughter. They have found that laughter releases endorphins, brain chemicals that reduce pain and induce euphoria. Laughter also enhances immune function, and lowers blood pressure by causing blood vessels to dilate—and, as Swami Beyondananda has said, this is certainly better than having them die early.

Laughter is indeed medicine, and not just in the palliative sense. Laughter is medicine in the Native American sense, a form of magic which used wisely can transmute tension into release, pain into insight, rigidity into flexibility and separation into connectedness. At times of transition and re-examination—as midlife no doubt is—humor can be a valuable tool for releasing the past and designing the future.

One of my favorite stories—supposedly true—illustrates the deeper powers of humor as a tool for transformation. During the Cuban missile crisis, Soviet and American negotiators were deadlocked, and there was tremendous tension in the room. Finally, one of the Soviet delegates suggested they each go around and tell a joke. He volunteered the first one: "What is the difference between capitalism and communism? In capitalism, man exploits man. In communism, it's the other way around." Everyone laughed, the tension was released, and they were able to continue the meeting. In a magical instant, laughter helped the negotiators rise above the duality of *us vs. them* and reminded them of the human heart we share in common.

Midlife crisis or midlife opportunity?

The passage known as midlife presents a great opportunity to reflect upon, re-evaluate, redefine, and redesign our lives. My cohort Swami Beyondananda refers to midlife as "intermission"—a break between the first and second acts of life where you consider your "mission" for the first half, and choose the same or a new mission for the second. For example, a woman might find that her first half mission was raising a family—and now wants to turn her attention to business or the creative arts. In contrast, there's the friend of mine who spent the first half of his adult life pursuing career and dodging commitment, and now is delighted to be a dad for the first time at age forty-eight. In making any choice—even an obvious choice for the better—there is often sadness for whatever is being left behind and fear of the unknown that lies ahead. Laughter is an excellent way to acknowledge, accept and release these inevitable feelings, and to give us perspective on our situation.

Years ago, I decided to make a career change from freelance writer to full-time humorist. My intention in this regard must have been very strong, because all of my writing jobs dried up instantly. I used to joke that I was going through what I called my "baroque period"—so baroque, I was Haydn from the landlord—but after a while I sunk into a funk that even this joke couldn't cure. My wife Trudy and I were two months behind in our rent, and it simply wasn't funny. Looking for some kind of spiritual anchor in our lives, we started each day reading a passage from "A Course In Miracles." At the time, I just didn't see how reading spiritual truisms could possibly help us through our very material problem. One morning, the lesson we read was "You are not upset for the reason you think." For some reason, that one really pushed my buttons. I knew very well why I was upset. We had no money and couldn't pay our rent!

I was just about to launch into a full-blown "tantrum yoga" rant when the phone rang. Trudy answered, and then put her hand over the receiver. "Steve," she whispered. "It's the landlord. What should I tell him?"

I thought for a couple of seconds, and then it came to me. "How about, 'you're not upset for the reason you think?'"

Trudy and I both burst out laughing—I don't remember if we shared the joke with the landlord—but something changed with that outburst of laughter. Swami Beyondananda often talks about a "good laughsitive," and I think that's what this was. Not only did the explosion of laughter help us release tension, but that little joke helped us surrender control over a situation we had little control over anyway. The laughter reminded us we were bigger than our problem and for the first time, our financial situation didn't seem so overwhelming. We still had some difficulty for a few months, but we were more relaxed, more able to enjoy our career transition as an *adventure* instead of an ordeal. Whenever we found ourselves lapsing into despair or self-pity, we would remember this joke, and "regularhilarity" would be restored. We found ourselves paraphrasing those 60s icons, the Fabulous Furry Freak Brothers: "Laughter will get you through times of no money better than money will get you through times of no laughter." In other words, whenever we are faced with adversity, one of the best ways to overcome gravity is with levity.

Even in our darkest moments—or perhaps especially in those dire situations—laughter may be the only way to let in *the light*. In his book, *Man's Search for Meaning*, Dr. Viktor Frankl recalls his experiences as an inmate in a Nazi death camp. He and a fellow inmate made a pact—each day, they would make each other laugh by imagining themselves years in the future looking back on the experience. Not only did this perspective help remove them temporarily from the pain of everyday life, but it afforded them the most human response of laughter in the most inhuman of circumstances.

In a setting where inmates were stripped of all dignity and much of their humanity, being able to laugh created a spiritual *reserve*—a place where their captors had no control over them. I am reminded of a delightful *Far Side* cartoon set in Hell. There is fire and brimstone everywhere, devils with pitchforks poking the poor unfortunates, and in the midst of this scene there is a fellow wheeling a wheelbarrow and blithely whistling. One of the devils is saying to the other, "I don't think we're getting through to that guy."

Similarly, some death camp inmates learned to use humor to gain a small degree of leverage in an impossible situation. A joke told in the camps at that time illustrates how humor can—at least for the moment—turn power relationships upside down. Two Jews decide to assassinate Hitler. They know that his motorcade passes a particular intersection each day at 11:00 a.m., and so they lie in wait for the Führer. 11:00 a.m. comes and goes, and Hitler does not arrive. 11:15. 11:30, and still no Hitler. Finally, at 11:45, one of the would-be assassins turns to the other and says, "Gee, I hope nothing's happened to him."

Even in the inevitable transition from this world to the next, laughter represents the triumph of the human spirit. A family member recently died at the age of 94. He had always been the kind of person who could light up a room with a good-hearted joke or quip. His memorial service carried on that legacy. He had written a eulogy for himself which ended with the famous Woody Allen remark: "I'm not afraid of dying. I just don't want to be there when it happens."

Friends and family left that memorial service happier and brighter, empowered to face whatever passages that loomed in their own lives. Likewise, you can make laughter a healing force in your own life—physically, emotionally, mentally and spiritually—as you segue into your own second act. Let's take a deeper look at four ways humor can help turn your midlife crisis into midlife opportunity—and some techniques for using laughter to bring physical healing, emotional release, mental flexibility and spiritual perspective.

Laughter and physical well-being

As I mentioned earlier, laughter has some proven health benefits. For those at any stage in life, laughter is perhaps the one thing that can make us look and feel younger instantly! Years ago, my favorite uncle—then in his late 80s—was in the hospital. He wasn't doing well and had sunk into depression. Since I lived six hundred miles away and couldn't visit him in person, I decided to call him on the phone. I was a bit reluctant because I was afraid I'd begin talking with him and become as depressed as he was. The moment he answered the phone, a joke magically sprung to mind. I told him about a man who needed a serious operation, and so he went to the finest surgeon in the country. The surgery was successful, but when the surgeon presented the bill, the patient told him he couldn't pay it.

"What about your health insurance?" the doctor said.

"I don't have any," the man replied.

Exasperated, the surgeon said, "OK, just pay what you can."

"I'm sorry," the patient told him, "but I can't pay anything. I haven't got a cent to my name."

Now the surgeon was livid. "If you knew you couldn't pay, why did you come to the finest surgeon in the country?"

"Because," said the man, "when it comes to my health, money is no object!"

My uncle laughed uproariously—this was, after all, a joke on the very medical system that held his own fate in the balance—and then he told me one.

Mid-Laugh Opportunity

A world-renowned rabbi and New York City cab driver both died and arrived at the Pearly Gates at the same time. The cab driver was ushered in immediately, but the rabbi was left waiting outside. For hours he waited, and finally impatience got the best of him. He approached the attending angel and demanded, "Look here, I'm a man of God. How can you let that cab driver in so quickly and leave me waiting out here?"

"It's simple," replied the angel. "When you expounded on the Talmud, everyone slept. But when he drove, everyone prayed."

Now it was my turn to laugh. Back and forth we went for over twenty minutes, and by the time I hung up the phone, my uncle's voice was rich with vitality and good cheer. And I felt pretty good too. Later in the day, I got a call from my brother, who happened to be in New York and had visited my uncle after the phone call. "What did you do to Uncle Barney?" he asked. "This is the best shape he's been in in weeks!"

Innocent laughter coaxes out our child-like nature, even if it's been buried for years. My friends were walking with their young daughter through a seedy part of town. Totally guileless, the little girl started a conversation with a gruff biker type who was standing on a street corner. "Hello," she said cheerfully, "what's your name?"

Determined to give her the brush-off, he said, "It starts with an 'M'."

"So does mine!" said the girl.

Of course, the biker was drawn in. "So what's your name?" he asked.

"Emily!" she said proudly.

The man's hardened face broke into a smile, and he started to laugh. "Did you hear that?" he called out to a crony. "Emily begins with M!" And as the family walked away, he was still laughing, for a brief moment an innocent little boy once again.

All of us suffer from "humorrhoids" from time to time, that hardening of attitudes which makes us feel and look older than we really are—and professional humorists are no exception. My wife Trudy has a beautifully brilliant way to bump me out of bad moods. She becomes the Energizer Bunny. She gets a goofy expression on her face, turns her head slightly to the side, and does a very rapid Charley Chaplin walk in my direction. If I try to push her away or turn her around, she turns like a wind-up toy and keeps coming. Inevitably, I break down with laughter in the face of this relentless, good-natured devotion that is unstoppable. This is, as a matter of fact, a terrific metaphor for the loving nature of existence. As the dyslexic paranoid might say, the Universe is plotting to make us happy—and there isn't a thing we can do about it!

By the time most of us reach midlife, the cultural mindset (what visionary astrologer Caroline Casey calls "the reality police") has so firmly established itself that we are convinced that life is serious business. We have already learned to *think our way* out of problems, and consequently we think too much—and completely overlook the simple, practical solutions staring us in the face. Like the cartoon I saw on a bulletin board in (where else?) a California bookstore. In the first panel of the cartoon, a boy is caught in a raging river and is calling out to his dog, "Lassie! Get help!" The second panel shows Lassie on a psychiatrist's couch.

Paradoxically, the most physical of humor can be the most spiritual as well—because it transcends boundaries of language and culture. As Victor Borge has said, laughter is the shortest distance between two people. Several years ago, my friend Alan and I went to a Tibetan art exhibit in San Francisco. There were several actual Tibetan Buddhist monks there, and most of the folks stood in awkward awe of them. Not Alan. He went right up to one and began a conversation. And, it turned out, the monk was what the Swami would call a "Fu Ling master." Describing the political situation in Tibet, he said in halting English, "Very dangerous. No 911."

Later on, Alan and I were in the gift shop, where he was looking to buy a purse for his girlfriend. Now I have a habit that I've never gotten over, dating back to when I was an impish child. Anything that could possibly be considered a "hat" I put on my head—colanders (terrific World War I helmets), toilet seat covers (they make great floppy "berets"), anything head-sized. I looked at the soft cloth purse Alan had in his hands, and I impulsively put one on my head. Alan followed suit. Within seconds, the monk was at our side with a purse on his head too. I looked at the other museum-goers looking at the monk, and I realized that this small and elegant gesture forever changed their perspective about God being *serious*.

Laughter is truly an "in-body" experience that gives us the physical experience of joy that all of those scriptures talk about. So how can we embody laughter on a daily basis? Here is a simple exercise from Swami Beyondananda's book, *Duck Soup for the Soul*, to bring you through the "fool range" of laughter:

At the first sign of "irregularhilarity," begin with a big guffaw, making the sound HOO HOO HOO, coming from the base of the body. Even if nothing feels funny, make the sound. Any time things don't feel funny is the best time to laugh!

Next, move up to the solar plexus and give forth with a good belly laugh—HO HO HO. Did you know that laughing at your belly reduces shame and makes food taste better?

Next, make the vowel sound "ah" with a HA HA HA— a good hearty laugh coming from the heart.

Then on up to the throat with a chuckle—HEH HEH HEH. Depending on your age, the laugh will remind you of Steve Allen—or Beavis and Butthead.

Finally, move your awareness up to the middle of your forehead and titter, HEE HEE HEE. Indeed, you are tittering on the edge of enlightenment.

When you've done that, reverse the vowel sounds, moving downward through all of the laugh centers. As the Swami says, there's nothing like a good vowel movement to clear the pipes and extend your laugh span.

Laughter and emotional release

A psychotherapist friend of mine—who prides herself on her level of caring and involvement—had undergone a particularly stressful week. As we talked on the phone, I decided to share a story with her.

Two psychiatrists each had their practice in the same building for twenty-five years, but had never spoken. After a quarter century in practice, one of them still appeared young and upbeat. The other looked old and beat up. One day, they found themselves on the elevator together. Unable to contain his curiosity, the prematurely-aged psychiatrist began a conversation with his colleague. "I've got to know," he began. "How can you spend twenty-five years listening to people's problems and still look so bright and cheerful?"

"Who listens?" was the reply.

My friend exploded in laughter—I wish I could have seen her face when the joke "detonated"—and her tone of voice changed for the rest of the conversation. As I reflected on this "random act of comedy," I realized that the joke allowed this very conscientious therapist to be vicariously *naughty*. While she herself would feel very guilty if her mind drifted even a little while in session with a patient, she was able to thoroughly enjoy imagining what it would be like to give her overly-demanding patients the proverbial *finger*. This kind of periodic emotional release through humor is almost a necessity for anyone who must deal with tragedy and distress on a daily basis—doctors, nurses, EMS workers, firefighters, police. In fact, a study several years ago at Rush Presbyterian Medical Center in Chicago concluded that EMS workers who could not use humor in this way were far more likely to burn out than those who relied on *dark humor* to get them through difficult moments.

So what does this emotional release have to do with midlife? Simply this: Like any passage, physical or metaphorical, you can only take a certain amount of baggage along. Laughter helps release excess emotional baggage and heal suffering that no longer serves a useful purpose. The sweetness of laughter can help us face unlovable parts of ourselves and our lives, and keep feelings from hardening into chronic patterns such as depression, rage and anxiety. Wholehearted laughter can also give us the perspective to forgive those who have wronged us, and allow us to move on in peace.

One of the best illustrations of how laughter and emotional health go together is the movie, *Prince of Tides*. As the film begins, the character played by Nick Nolte is emotionally shut down and paralyzed by unacknowledged rage. He has a sense of humor, but his jokes are like grenades lobbed over a stone wall—they are angry, aggressive, designed to keep people away and discourage intimacy. As his therapy progresses and he begins to face the truth about his dysfunctional upbringing, an interesting thing happens. He is able to find humor in the absurd entanglements in his family. Along with the pain, he remembers genuinely humorous moments in his childhood, and is able to laugh wholeheartedly about them. By the end of the film, he has developed a *spiritual maturity* in which he is able to accept his life, release blame, and live in the present rather than being stuck in the past.

All of us have these shadow parts of our lives, and laughter can help us gain perspective and healing. I spent eleven years of my childhood in a housing project in Brooklyn, and all I can say is, "Thank God for humor." When bigger kids would try to shake me down for cash, I learned to say, "I live here. If I had any money, would I be living here?" For the most part, the older kids laughed and left me alone. After all, I was a prodigy: Eight years old and I was already doing comedy for money!

I recently read a book about Feng Shui, the Chinese art of placement and beauty. That's when I realized that I grew up in a dys-Fengshui-nal household—everything was ugly and brought bad luck! Somehow, being able to laugh at this painful part of my own childhood—and watching others enjoy laughing at it as well—heals and releases some of the stored up pain.

Another aspect of my childhood that has definitely required healing is growing up with an over-anxious Jewish mother. Joking about her—with only slight exaggeration—has allowed me to entertain others while I heal myself. The archetypal Jewish mother is a great cook who worries about everything. Well, my mom worried about everything—except her cooking, which could have benefited from a little concern. Finally, when I was about ten she went to work and stopped cooking entirely. At school, I proudly told classmates that all our meals were now being prepared by a world famous chef—Chef Boy Ar Dee.

Although her cooking never would have gotten her to the major leagues, she was elected to the Worrier's Hall of Fame on the first ballot. I swear to you, this really happened: Back in the 70s, I took a job doing tree work. My job was to tag, and then help remove trees that had Dutch elm disease. My mother was actually afraid that I would catch Dutch elm disease! "Mom," I patiently explained, "people can't get Dutch elm disease. Dogs can get it, though."

"Dogs get it?" she asked anxiously (she was concerned about Buster). "What happens to dogs?"

"They lose their bark," I replied.

Every time someone laughs at this story, a little bit of my childhood heals.

Laughter also can help us heal the judgments that keep us from being kinder to others—and ourselves. There's a story I like to tell—especially to church groups—about a little town in West Texas many years ago. The town madam came to the minister with an offer. "I want to make amends for my life and donate everything I have to build a new chapel."

"Well, ma'am," replied the minister, "I need to think about it. Come back tomorrow."

The next day she returned and the minister had made his decision. "I'm sorry, ma'am, but I can't accept your offer."

The woman left and one of the townspeople who had been listening in approached the minister. "Reverend," he said, "we need a new building. Why did you turn down the woman's generous offer?"

"Because her money," replied the minister, "is tainted money."

"What do you mean, her money," the man replied. "It's our money."

It's amazing to look out at a crowd of faces and watch people laugh at that joke—as everyone always does. I see faces lighten and brighten as folks are relieved of the burden of self-righteousness.

Years ago, I was the emcee at an outdoor music event. One of the performers was a very talented harp player who was herself a little tightly strung. Shortly before she was to go on, we needed to make a sudden change in the program. One of the other performers had to get to another engagement and needed to go on first. Instead of cheerfully accommodating the other musician, the harp player flew into a rage at the change. Unfortunately, the audience saw her outburst and decided they didn't like her. Finally it was her turn to perform. Seeking to soften the situation somewhat, I asked if she minded if I "channeled" Ed Sullivan to introduce her. She was absorbed in her own thoughts and mumbled, "whatever."

In my finest Ed Sullivan style, I introduced her. "Right now on our sho-o-ow, for you music lovers, please welcome—"

Despite my enthusiasm, she got only tepid applause. And once onstage, she proceeded to tune up for what seemed like ten minutes. Now the audience really hated her! Finally, she was ready to play. Just as her fingers were about to touch the harp to play her first note, Ed Sullivan boomed: "WASN'T SHE WUNNERFUL, FOLKS? LET'S HEAR IT FOR HER!"

The audience burst into laughter, and with the laughter the tension evaporated. Released from their negative feelings about her, the audience was now ready to hear the harp player's music. The laughter seemed to dissolve her nervousness as well, and she played a beautiful set to a raptly attentive audience. And when she was done, she received warm, heartfelt applause.

Laughter can also release long-standing emotional pain. At one of my humor workshops several years ago, we were relating embarrassing moments that were traumatic at the time, but could now be laughed at. One participant, a therapist, told the following story. When he began his practice, one of his first clients was a young woman who had been sexually molested by her grandfather. Aware of the very sensitive nature of the situation, the therapist gently and tentatively questioned the young woman. "And when did your grandfather molest you?" he asked.

"Before he died," replied the woman.

For some reason this struck the therapist as hilariously funny, and, in spite of himself, he burst out laughing. The more he tried to control his laughter, the harder he laughed. Soon, the young woman was laughing too, and before long her laughter gave way to tears. Thanks to this emotional release, she was finally able to talk about the traumatic situation for the first time.

Sometimes the Universe will create what the Swami calls "farce fields" where a healing joke shows up and magically heals emotional distress. Many years ago, back when I was a long-haired hippie-radical, a friend and I were driving across country. It was a great trip until we got to Denver. We went into a Denny's and they refused to serve us because of our long hair. With uncharacteristic fury, we silently vowed to return after dark and throw a brick through their window. Still fuming, we pulled into a gas station for a fill up. The attendant took one look at us and shouted, "Go away. We don't serve no homo sapiens here!"

My friend and I looked at each other and burst out laughing. And with the laughter, all desire for revenge vanished. How could we possibly wish any harm to such absurdly ignorant folks? Instead of a broken window (and possibly a night in jail and a free haircut) to remember our experience by, we now have a great story that spreads healing laughter each time we retell it.

In fact, humor is a marvelous outlet for harmlessly expressing anger and frustration. A few years ago, I purchased an educational video. One of the narrators was an English woman with a very, very irritating vocal quirk. From time to time—and for no apparent reason—her voice would rise to a near-screech that was to me like fingernails on a chalkboard. I would be watching the tape, listening to her, and with no warning her voice would do this. It was making me crazy. Here I was, not even a third of the way through the tape series, and I wanted to throw the tapes away—and do bodily harm to the narrator. In the midst of my irritation, I got a mischievous idea. I fast-forwarded the tape to a place near the end where the narrator was arising from her chair. I picked the point that looked to me to be the most uncomfortable position for her to be stuck in—kind of hunched over with a pained expression on her face. I pressed "pause" and left her frozen in that position. After about twenty minutes, my wife Trudy gently suggested that maybe I should release her and let the tape go forward. "No!" I said. "She must be punished!"

After about forty-five minutes, I decided the poor woman had suffered enough, and proceeded with the video. Interestingly, her voice never bothered me again.

Up until now, I've talked about midlife as a time where we ourselves choose to make a positive change. But quite often, it feels as if the changes have chosen us. Dealing with fragile, aging parents or our own health challenges, feeling the emptiness of a career that is no longer satisfying, undergoing financial hardship or loss of a relationship may not initially seem like a great source of mirth and humor. But when we voluntarily choose to laugh at adversity, we free up emotional energy and find ourselves more in the flow. Here are some techniques for using laughter to release toxic emotions so we don't take things too "poisonally."

1. *Laugh In Your Own Face.* Some years ago, my friend Jim arrived at his real estate office and found his partner had gone bankrupt. Jim had lost $90,000 (a substantial sum back in the 70s) and was not amused. He walked into the

men's room and instead of slitting his wrists (his first fleeting impulse), he stood staring at his unhappy puss in the mirror. Mockingly, he began to laugh. Ha, ha, ha. Ha, ha, ha. Ha, ha, HA! Within moments, he was laughing for real. After a few minutes of hearty release, he called his wife and took her to lunch to "celebrate." He never looked back in either anger or hurt, and has gone on to great financial success.

Not all of us would be as ready to laugh as Jim, so we might consider having some props around to make it easier. Personally, I love those Groucho nose-glasses-mustache things. What an enlightening experience to recite one's problems wearing one of those devices while looking in the mirror. If you can use a super-high Mickey Mouse voice or a low Bullwinkle voice, all the better. This is guaranteed to cure even the most stubborn case of humorrhoids.

2. *Sing the Blues.* The blues was invented for a very specific healing purpose—to release sadness and frustration in a situation where you have little or no control. The energy of singing—especially when combined with exaggerated humor—is an excellent way to release emotional tension in a physical way. A few years ago, a friend of mine was enduring a visit by her mother, a harshly critical and emotionally cold person. My friend came over one afternoon lamenting her situation, likening her mom to the *wire mother* in the classic Harlow monkey experiments. (As you may remember from college psychology, those monkeys raised by *wire mothers*—a wire frame with a milk bottle—failed to thrive.) A musician friend was also there with his guitar, and we spontaneously wrote "The Wire Mother Blues." My friend rapped, raved and wailed about how horrible her mother was, and left with a big smile on her face. The next day, she called to say what a *healing* this blues song was and how much easier it was now to be with her mother!

3. *Enjoy Your Suffering.* A few years ago, I was at a weeklong retreat where I absolutely hated the food. Since

there was little I could do about the food (other than not eat it), I decided to really enjoy not liking it. Each meal, I came up with fresh comedy material about the food, usually beginning with "You know what I love about this food?" ("You know what I love about this food? I'm really going to enjoy the airline food on the way home.") The first thing that happened was people would purposely sit with me at mealtime, just to hear me creatively complain. The second thing that happened was even more surprising. After three or four days, I lost all energy for complaining. At each meal, I would gratefully choose the food items I wanted to eat and forget about the rest. And by the end of the week, I was actually enjoying the food.

Laughter and mental flexibility

Swami Beyondananda has said, "The only thing certain in life is uncertainty, and come to think of it, I'm not even sure that is true." Certainly the changes in midlife can bring uncertainty, and there's nothing like humor to help us develop the flexibility to release old mental habits and find new ways of seeing, for laughter is indeed a mind-altering substance. A good paradoxical joke can wrestle the mind to the ground and allow surrender to a deeper reality.

There's an old story about a reporter interviewing Albert Einstein at his laboratory in Princeton, New Jersey. The reporter was surprised to see a large horseshoe hanging over the professor's office doorway. "Professor Einstein," she asked, "you're a great scientist. Surely you don't believe a horseshoe will bring good luck."

"Of course I don't," he replied.

"Then why is the horseshoe up there?" the reporter insisted.

"Because it works whether you believe it or not."

For centuries, Zen masters have been using the *koan* to trick the logical mind and elicit moments of enlightenment. Like the classic, "What is the sound of one hand clapping?" paradox forces the mind off of its usual pathways and offers a glimpse of the infinite. Years ago, when I was teaching a group of sixth graders, I had a placard hanging from the classroom ceiling. On one side of the card, it said, "The statement on the other side of this card is true." On the other side it said: "The statement on the other side of this card is false." You can't imagine the hours of entertainment and discussion that ensued as the kids puzzled over that conundrum.

One of the Swami's favorite ruses over the years has been to tell audiences that to have successful relationships, one must avoid judging and blame. "I think people who judge are TERRIBLE!" says the Swami, "and those who blame are the cause of all the world's problems!"

Of course, everyone laughs because their own belief system—open-minded and tolerant as it may be—is still a prison of sorts. Several years ago, my wife and I attended a conference at a very, very politically correct college campus. We stayed in a dormitory and were astounded to see a sign proclaiming that any "racist, sexist, or homophobic remarks" would not be tolerated. I wonder if anyone recognized the irony in the inference that "Intolerance will not be tolerated!" In fact, what I call "pumping ironies"— pointing out and exaggerating ironies so that the inherent contradictions can no longer stay hidden—is an excellent way to help release us from the prison of absolutist thinking and the trance of "I'm right, and you're wrong." It's no accident that one of the first things Hitler did when he came to power was arrest the cabaret comedians. He feared them more than he did Nazism's serious critics because of the power laughter and comedy have to shine the light of truth on unexamined beliefs and break the trance of authoritarianism.

About ten years ago, I was on a festival program with Country Joe McDonald of the old '60s band, Country Joe and the Fish. He started out doing some of his newer material, but it wasn't until he sang his classic *Feel Like I'm Fixin' To Die Rag* that the crowd came alive. It was a bitterly ironic anti-war song ("Be the first one on your block to have your boy come home in a box.") that galvanized sentiment against the Vietnam War in the late 1960s. As I watched the audience—hippies and straights alike—enthusiastically sing along more than twenty years later, I realized that this song probably did more to transform our mindset about the war than any speech or article ever could have.

Humor has the power to dissolve not just political trances, but to shake us off of habitual mental pathways that have limited our thinking. In fact, a joke can be a delightful dance with the invisible, a voluntary *mini-trance* resulting in a *mini-enlightenment*. In his book *Trances People Live*, psychologist Stephen Wolinsky describes two characteristics of a trance state, both of which apply to hearing a joke. First, there is a narrowed focus of attention. Imagine you are in an elevator or in a crowd in front of a movie theater. You overhear someone telling a joke you haven't heard: "so these two cannibals are eating a clown..." and immediately the joke-teller has your full attention. For a moment you forget about the situation you had just been obsessing about or the hot (or cold) weather, and possibly even an attractive individual you'd been glancing at. You are utterly focused on eavesdropping on the joke until you are released from the *trance* by the punch line—"and one of them says to the other, 'Say does this taste funny to you?'"

The second characteristic of trance is suspension of disbelief. In listening to a joke, you respectfully ask your critical mind to *disappear* until the moment of the punch line. You don't say to yourself, "That's ridiculous. Cannibals don't eat clowns." Instead, you choose to cheerfully play by the rules of humor where anything goes and things that don't belong together get thrust together in new alignments. In the context of a Gary Larson cartoon, it is perfectly sane for animals to talk. In contrast, the individual who writes an irate letter to the newspaper complaining that they are misleading the public and misrepresenting reality by showing talking animals is the one who would be considered "marble-deficient."

Like the magician who deftly commands and diverts our attention until the proverbial rabbit gets pulled out of the hat, an adept joke teller draws us in and keeps us away from the punch line until the right moment. A man tells he wife he is going down to the corner bar to buy a pack of cigarettes. While he is standing in line waiting to get change for the cigarette machine, he notices an attractive woman at the bar gesturing towards him. He tries to ignore her, but finally, overcome by curiosity, he goes over to see what she wants. "I want to buy you a drink," she says. He explains that he's married, and his wife is waiting for him, but she insists. "Okay," he says, and lets her buy him a drink. To make a long story shorter, she buys him eight drinks.

Finally, he shakily stands up and says, "I really must leave now. My wife—"

But the woman cuts him off and asks him to come home with her and make love. Again, he protests, but there is something so compelling about this woman that he goes home with her. They make love, he falls asleep, and all of a sudden awakens with a start. It's 2:00 a.m. He quickly pulls his clothes on and wakes his companion. "Do you have any talcum powder?" he asks. He takes the talcum powder, rubs it on his hands and goes home.

His wife is waiting for him, fuming. "Where were you?" she demands.

"Well," he says, "you're not going to believe this. While I was waiting for change, this woman at the bar motioned to me. I don't know what possessed me to go over there but I did. Anyway, she bought me a drink—eight drinks, actually—and asked me to come home with her. I must have been crazy, but I did. We made love, I fell asleep, and when I woke up I came home as quickly as I could."

"Let me see your hands," his wife says suspiciously. He extended his powdered hands. "Just as I thought, you liar!" she says. "You were out bowling with the boys, weren't you?"

If you reacted like I did the first time I heard this joke, you exploded with laughter, delight and surprise. I had been so totally drawn into the narrative that the punch line came as a complete surprise to me. In this sense, a joke is very much like life—we get so involved in the story that we don't see the punch line coming. Like the small child gleefully playing peekaboo, we delight in the surprise as the invisible becomes visible. The playful mind offers us a new way of seeing and thinking. Comedy is like playing peekaboo with the logical mind, reminding us to recognize hidden parts—and hidden solutions. One of my favorite ways of "committing random acts of comedy" is by earnestly absorbing myself in a *serious* conversation, then veering off in an unexpected direction. I was at a weekend workshop, and found myself talking to a woman who had not been in a relationship for a long time. "I've been celibate for the past nine months," she confided, a little sadly.

I nodded, and said earnestly, "You know, I was celibate for fourteen years." She looked at me with a mixture of awe and respect, and I continued, "but when I turned fifteen, I said, 'Enough of that.'" Of course, she burst out laughing, delighted in being tricked out of her sad mood. This kind of switch in context—you think you are going here, but you are really headed there—is a key ingredient in creative thinking, and success. A few years ago, we met a very successful artist at a crafts show, and he told us his story. He had accidentally spilled some latex paint on his studio floor one evening, and when he returned in the morning, he noticed that the spilled latex had dried in the shape of a tie. This gave him an idea. He crafted some scraps of rubber into palm trees and pink flamingoes, painted them, and attached them to the "tie." In a matter of months, he was making hilarious, playful rubber, 3-D ties in every shape, color and theme imaginable. Since that time, he has hired other artists to help him—and still can't keep up with the demand.

More and more, people are putting the mind in its proper place—as a creative servant of the heart, rather than a ruler bent on control. One of the important pieces of wisdom that we glean by midlife (or sooner, if we're fortunate) is that being in the flow works far better than being in control. Humor and laughter can give us the mental flexibility to put us in the flow of creativity. The following humor-cultivating practices can help you use the mind to generate creative options rather than to obsess, worry and control.

1. *Pumping Ironies.* Swami Beyondananda has uncovered a debilitating mental condition that keeps us from truly using our power—irony deficiency. Seeing a doctor won't help, Swami says, but seeing a paradox will. Irony deficiency results not so much from lack of irony in our lives—ironies abound in our insane society—but rather from our inability to see or process these ironies. How else could a "freedom-loving" country such as the U.S. have more people behind bars than any other country in the free world? Or spend nearly 50 percent of its resources on weapons of destruction? Or have an environmental *debate* on whether or not we should be destroying our planet? As we pump these ironies—bring them to consciousness through humorous exaggeration—we take the first step at resolving the glaring contradictions in our culture and our own lives.

The simplest irony is the oxymoron, which can be as innocent as *jumbo shrimp* or as tragic as *holy war.* I suggest you find yourself a list of oxymora—they seem to be circulating all over the web—and see if you can add a few of your own. Next, look to your own life and begin to notice incongruities that you can bring to light through humor. You might begin with the phrase, "How come?" "How come I am so insanely busy during my leisure time?" "How come I spend almost as much on child care as I earn after taxes on my job?" "How come I am willing to drive around aimlessly for forty-five minutes rather than *waste time* asking for directions?" As we bring paradox to consciousness, we are more likely to see solutions that fall outside the box of our normal thinking.

A few years ago, I was giving a talk on humor and offered up another irony: Pro-Life advocates who support the death penalty. After my talk an irate woman came up to me, upset that I criticized the anti-abortion movement. Seeing she was stuck, I told her I had recently watched a TV show where three religious leaders discussed the issue of when life actually begins. The priest said that life begins at conception. Oblivious to the fact that I was telling her a joke, she nodded in agreement with the priest. Then they asked the minister, and he said that life begins when the infant takes the first breath. And there was the woman, totally absorbed in the story, shaking her head *no*. Finally, they asked the rabbi, "Rabbi, when does life begin?"

"Life begins," he said, "when the children leave home and the dog dies."

In spite of herself, the woman burst out laughing, at once lightened and enlightened. Not that I changed her mind. But for the moment when levity allowed us both to rise above the dueling dualities of Pro Life vs. Pro Choice, there was a change of heart.

2. *Reframing.* Reframing is a shift in context that allows us to look at a situation in a more useful way. Calling it "midlife opportunity" rather than "midlife crisis" is a particularly helpful reframe, because it empowers us to seek creative options rather than stay stuck in the problem. Singer-songwriter Jana Stanfield's tune, *I'm Not Lost, I'm Exploring* has helped countless listeners reframe overt chaos as covert growth. Perhaps the master of reframe was the gifted hypnotherapist, Dr. Milton Erickson, whose work was the foundation of what is now called Neurolinguistic Programming (NLP). When Erickson was a young resident at a psychiatric hospital, one of the inmates had delusions of being Jesus Christ. One day, Erickson approached him and said, "I understand you have some experience as a carpenter." The man, of course, could not contradict this suggestion without denying his delusion—and went on to become a competent woodworker.

One of my favorite reframing stories involves two seminary students who share the same secret vice—smoking cigarettes. Finally, torn by guilt, they decide they must ask the monsignor permission to smoke. Each does this, and when they compare notes they are puzzled to find the monsignor has given them contradictory answers. "I don't understand it," said the first. "I asked, 'Monsignor, is it okay for me to smoke while I'm praying?' and he said, 'Certainly not.'"

"That's funny," said the second. "I asked if it was okay if I prayed while I was smoking and he said, 'Of course.'"

Reframing can change—and even save—your life. At the age of 32, Buckminster Fuller was a failure at business. Facing bankruptcy with a wife and young child, he stood overlooking Lake Michigan with the intention of ending his life. As he contemplated his fate, a wild thought came to him. If he was going to throw his life away, why didn't he at least *donate it to science*? At that moment, he drew away from self-destruction and vowed to give his life in service to the world. He went on to live another fifty-five productive years as a philosopher, scientist and inventor. Among other things, he gave the world the geodesic dome and the concept of *spaceship earth*.

How can you humorously reframe your challenges and failings? As the Swami says, "Never, never, never call yourself a failure. Instead say, 'I am tremendously successful at failing.'" Taking a cue from Jana Stanfield, fill in the blanks: "I'm not _____, I'm _____." Once you learn how easily the mind can be outwitted, you will learn to outwit it yourself!

3. *Seeing With A Child's Eye.* I was at a weekend retreat a few years back, and I noticed a five-year-old with one of the local dogs. He had the dog's tail in his hand and was furtively waving the tail back and forth. "What are you doing?" I asked. "I want the dog to be happy," the boy replied.

In the child's mind, this syllogism made sense. A dog wags his tail when he is happy, therefore I can make him happy by wagging his tail. The humor in these logical gaffes is endless; Art Linkletter made a career of interviewing children on *Kids Say the Darndest Things*.

In contrast, deadpan comedian Stephen Wright has made a career out of thinking like a child. When asked how he creates his comedy, Wright replied, "I try to see things from a child's perspective." This liberates him from the usual structures of reality and allows him to see underlying ideas and relationships which most of us miss. How else could he come up with the line: "I hate it when my foot falls asleep during the day. That means it's going to be up all night." Or his attempt to learn Spanish: "I bought one of those records that allows you to learn a foreign language while you sleep, but the record skipped, so now I can only stutter in Spanish."

Just for fun and enlightenment, practice seeing and hearing as a child does. In her book *Love Without End*, Glenda Green calls this "innocent perception." Perhaps the classic innocent perception story is *The Emperor's New Clothes*, in which the child's eyes could see while adults were blinded by convention and habit. A friend of mine was driving with his five-year-old on the Saturday before Christmas. As he made his way through stop-and-go traffic, he felt more and more stressed as he tried to complete his errands. At one point, another driver nudged in front of him, and that was the last straw. My friend loudly screamed invective at the driver who cut him off. After the outburst ended, his young son turned to him quietly and said, "Was that the Christmas spirit, dad?"

As he looked into his son's eyes, all perspective was restored. He spent the rest of the afternoon creeping through traffic in a state of joy and peace he hadn't felt for years.

Laughter and spiritual perspective

My favorite TV situation comedy was and still is *Seinfeld*. To me, the show was so original, so playfully daring, and so damned funny that in comparison everything else is just recycled *I Love Lucy*. I often wondered what it was exactly that made this show so compelling, and one day it came to me: *Seinfeld* is the most exquisite parody of human suffering that I've ever come across. In the Yiddish tradition, there are two comic archetypes—the *shlemiel* and the *shlamazel*. The *shlemiel* is the bumbling fool who spills soup on a hapless restaurant patron. The *shlamazel* (*mazel* in Yiddish is luck, *shlamazel* means bad luck) is the poor soul who is the recipient of spilled soup. Each *Seinfeld* episode was an intricate "waltz" of *shlemiel* and *shlamazel*, with the characters taking turns playing each of those roles. Time and time again, attempts to control reality—even with the best intentions—are inevitably thwarted as plans go awry. In this sense, the show that was supposedly about "Nothing" is really about *Everything*.

Buddha said that life is suffering, and at the root of suffering is attachment. If that's the case, *Seinfeld* probably has done more to further the understanding of Buddhist teaching than the Dalai Lama himself. George, clearly the most *attached* of the four main characters (i.e., the one whose happiness is most dependent on external conditions) is the one who suffers most. Kramer, the archetypal *shlemiel* who blithely goes through life hatching ridiculous schemes, seems to suffer least—because he is the least attached. George desperately looks for dates, and finds few. Jerry has no *charge* about meeting women so consequently dating is easy for him. But his attachment to *perfection* insures that he never finds the *right* girl. Elaine is attached to *looking good*—and so she is a magnet for embarrassing situations.

Just about every situation comedy from *I Love Lucy* onward is about attachment and the mind's futile attempts at control on the basis of limited knowledge. Lucy herself is obsessed with show business (attachment) and cooks up hare-brained plots (control), each with a glaring flaw that she fails to see until it is too late. What we are really seeing is a tragedy! But because of humorous exaggeration, a laugh track, and the fact it is happening to someone else and not us, we laugh. As Mel Brooks has said, "Tragedy is when I stub my toe. Comedy is when you fall down an open manhole and drown."

There is the classic joke about the two guys who meet on the street after not seeing each other for twenty-five years. "So how is your wife?" asks the first one.

"Don't ask, don't ask," says his friend in despair. "She left me—for another woman yet—and took everything I had."

"Could be worse," says the first gentleman. "But tell me, how's business?"

"Another terrible tragedy," says the hapless friend, shaking his head. "My business burned down, and it turns out my fire insurance had expired two days earlier, and I didn't know it. I lost it all."

"Could be worse," was the reply. "By the way, how's your son?"

At this the man heaved an audible sigh. "That, my friend, is the saddest tragedy of all. I had such great dreams for him. I imagined that one day he'd be saying, 'I would like to thank the Nobel Prize Committee...' Instead he's saying, 'You want fries with that?'"

"Could be worse," said the man once again.

At that point, the afflicted friend became furious. "Everything I say, you say, 'Could be worse, could be worse, could be worse.' How could it possibly be worse?"

"Could be happening to *me*," was the reply.

When we realize that the joke is always on us—even if it appears to be happening to someone else—we have taken a giant step away from suffering and towards compassion. And when we recognize that the best comedy is a parody of our own foolish attempts to force reality to bend to our own desires, we have achieved what Swami Beyondananda calls "fool realization." The "fooly-realized" being realizes that we are all fools, and there is nothing to do about it but surrender in joyful laughter.

To genuinely and wholeheartedly laugh at ourselves is a key step toward inner peace, outer freedom—and maybe even enlightenment. As some philosopher once said, "Life is far too important to be taken seriously." Consider the elderly neighbors or relatives whom you admire because they are not afraid to speak their mind or follow their heart. They have long since stopped caring what other folks think about them (having realized that most people don't think anyway), and instead spend their time delighting others in a way of their own choosing. Haven't you ever wished this freedom for yourself? Well, midlife—or wherever you are right now—is a great place to start. What if you didn't have to spend so much energy trying to look good or appear smart? What if you released trying to control the river, and instead became a part of the flow? How would your life improve if you were willing to risk appearing foolish?

As a comedian, I have definitely had to deal with this issue. It's like the cartoon I saw years ago. A clown is lying on a psychiatrist's couch and saying, "No one takes me seriously." For years, I performed as Swami wearing a rainbow clown wig—and yet I insisted I was not a *clown*. I even changed to the colorful turban I now wear to make this distinction—Swami is a wise guy, a commentator, *not* a fool to be laughed at. Last year, I found out otherwise. I was hired to perform in front of a group of rowdy women at a 60th birthday party. At one point in the performance, they began squirting me with that colorful, stringy stuff they sell in novelty stores. Although it does not stain or damage clothes, I was actually feeling assaulted by a gang of wild crones until I remembered to surrender to *the Farce*. Who did I think I was—of all people—to be exempt from ridicule? As I relaxed, I even began to enjoy this playful assault. I realized that volunteering to be a laughingstock released my own attachment to being in control—because after all, making people laugh is a form of control. (It's no coincidence that comedians will come backstage saying, "I killed 'em" or "I died" depending on the audience's reaction.) I have found since that time that, if I am even more *defenseless* as a performer and less bent on control, I have more deeply engaged audiences and enjoyed myself more.

Back when Polish jokes were first becoming popular in the 60s, I met a woman from Colombia. I was surprised to find that Colombians told the same jokes about the *Paztuzos*—some hapless out-group in that little country. Later in Texas, I heard *Aggie* jokes, and as a matter of fact, I have found that just about every culture projects "clue-deficiency" onto some poor group of people. The Yiddish tradition seems most functional to me in this regard. Jewish literature of the late 19th century features many wisely absurd stories about the mythical village of Chelm (or *Helm* if you have a problem with that guttural Germanic *ch* sound), where all the fools dwell. Since Chelm doesn't exist, one can tell Chelm stories with impunity without having some lug in a bar say, "Hey, fella, I'm from Chelm, and I take exception to that remark." The other advantage of citing an imaginary city of fools is that it becomes easier to realize the universality of foolishness; all of us from time to time qualify for citizenship in Chelm. Consequently, it becomes easier to laugh at our own foibles through others. That, I think, is the distinction between *laughing with* and *laughing at*. When we are *laughing at* we are saying, "Look at that stupid fool over there." When we *laugh with* we are saying, "That idiot I'm laughing at is me in disguise." In this sense, openhearted laughter can perform one of its loftiest spiritual functions—erasing the distinction between *I* and *thou*. When we see the truth in the old Firesign Theater line, "I think we're all bozos on this bus," we recognize our equality in the eyes of Creation. Since God is laughing at all of us equally, what's the point of trying to prove we're better than or smarter than someone else? And as we come to see the absurdity of attachment and control, we begin to let go of our white-knuckled grip on the steering wheel of life and reach for the joystick instead.

There are three spiritual-humorous practices which can ease your transition to the next phase of life and help create what the Swami calls "an alter-native reality" where whatever you are doing alters the natives for the better. These are defenselessness, celebration, and random acts of comedy.

1. Defenselessness. "A Course In Miracles," that spiritual text I had so much trouble with when I made my own career change, maintains that all human action is based either on love or on fear. Simplistic as it may sound, I have come to find this distinction very helpful. Openhearted laughter can create that small opening that allows us to move from the familiar trance of fear to the higher perspective of love. This is exactly what happened when the Soviet delegate told the joke about capitalism and communism. Because he told the joke on his own system as well, because he *disarmed* himself, he created the space for others to become defenseless too.

Another of my favorite stories—one that I have cherished since I was a youngster—involves the great baseball character, Casey Stengel. As the story goes, when Stengel was a rookie the fans in New York disliked him. Each time he walked onto the field or came up to bat, they booed. This went on for a while. And then one day, Casey walked onto the field to the usual chorus of boos. He tipped his cap, and a sparrow flew out from under his cap. The boos turned to laughter, the laughter to cheers, and he went on to become one of the most popular and beloved figures in New York history. So of course, the moral of the story is, if you're going to flip someone the bird—do it in a way that will make them laugh.

A few years ago, I returned from a trip and found an angry message on my answering machine. It seems I had made an agreement and then totally forgotten about it. The other individual was quite upset, and I wasn't sure what to do about it. I had definitely screwed up. Then I got a bright idea. I called him on the phone, and when he answered I began singing, "I'm Sorry." I sang the entire three-minute Brenda Lee song, including every "ho ho ho ho ho ho, oh yeah." When I was done, my colleague laughed, and we worked the situation out.

Creating defenselessness is not the same thing as allowing yourself to be the butt of cruel humor, but rather is an activity that requires high self-esteem. A workshop participant told of his early days as a firefighter. Being a Mormon who didn't smoke or drink—and being the *new guy*—he was singled out as the object of practical jokes and insult. He tried everything—ignoring the jokes, protesting to the fire department, returning the salvo with cruel jokes of his own—and nothing worked. He finally learned a better approach when a new *new guy* showed up. Naturally, the jokesters turned on the newer guy. But this *new guy's* response was to cheerfully laugh—and then take the joke on himself one step further. If, for example, one of the guys said, "Ah, your mother wears combat boots," he would reply, "That's why you guys should treat me better. Any of you ever get wakened in the morning by your mom tromping on your bed?" They quickly lost interest in taunting him.

In the martial arts form of *aikido*, you learn to move with the energy that is coming towards you instead of resisting the force. That way, there is nothing for the attacker to push up against, and the force is dissipated harmlessly. Defenseless humor works the same way. If you make yourself bigger than the insult and *absorb* it, it cannot hurt you.

Perhaps the first way of finding strength in defenselessness, is to do whatever it takes to remind yourself not to take life so seriously. When we take a step back from our circumstances and realize that life is a comedy of situations—and we are just having an episode—it is easier for us to take Swami Beyondananda's sage advice: "If life is a sitcom, may as well sit calm and enjoy it."

2. Celebration. I once asked a psychologist what she thought the most suppressed emotion was. Without hesitation, she responded, "Joy." Underneath all of the pain, stress and distress of life is a deep well of joy—and when laughter bubbles up from that well, it creates—wellness. Celebration is the joyful heart at play with others. In terms of sharing information, I am a great proponent of the internet, but when it comes to sharing love and laughter, there is nothing like the *outernet*—the web of family, friends, neighbors, co-workers and acquaintances we encounter daily.

In response to that classic new age question, "Do we create our own reality?" I have come to feel more and more that we *weave* our reality into the matrix of the greater reality. That's why *network* has become such a popular word. Because the next phase of our evolution seems to involve a network of peers weaving their dreams into a mutually beneficial, functional reality—this in contrast to the hierarchical structures that have defined our cultural reality in the past. In other words, in this future we are designing together, we will be able to be all that we can be—without joining the army.

To be in this state of celebration—as opposed to separation—involves acknowledging and accepting our differences, both individual and cultural. In a sense, we can learn to love even what we don't like. One of the great breakthroughs in beginning a real, heartfelt conversation on the subject of racism and intolerance was the TV show *All In the Family*. Archie Bunker verbalized our own unspoken xenophobic tendencies. He gave intolerance a human face, and consequently we could see parts of ourselves in him. At the same time, Archie gave folks *permission* to vent their own intolerant feelings and *play* with racial and ethnic stereotypes in a loving context. I have seen this myself during my stints at mostly-male workplaces. When there was trust and rapport, it was a great relief and release for us to kid each other about our racial or ethnic backgrounds—because it was done in the context of us all feeling a connection that transcended any of those labels.

In that spirit, I offer a description of heaven and hell as it would apply to the countries in Europe. In heaven, the police are English. The mechanics are German. The cooks are French. The lovers are Italian. And the whole thing is run by the Swiss. In hell, however, the police are German. The cooks are English. The mechanics are French. The lovers are Swiss. And it's all run by the Italians. I have told that joke hundreds of times in front of all kinds of audiences, and it is always received in the spirit it is offered—with love and appreciation.

Celebration also recognizes the inherently humorous nature of existence. A friend of mine who lived out in the country in Michigan found himself plagued by raccoons. They were breaking into his house, eating his garden and generally being a nuisance. His first impulse was, "Davy Crockett hats for everyone!" But he soon calmed down, and, being a humane kind of guy, went to the Humane Society and picked up some live traps. Apparently, if you capture the raccoons and drop them off somewhere ten or fifteen miles away, they won't come back. So my friend set out some traps and sure enough, the next morning each trap had a raccoon in it. He drove them to a place about fifteen miles away, dropped them off in the woods, and returned home. As he was pulling into his own driveway, there was someone else—with similar humane intentions—releasing raccoons on his land!

3. *Commit Random Acts of Comedy.* An acquaintance grew up in a small town in Illinois named Normal (those of you familiar with the area know I'm not making that up.) Just up the road from Normal was a much smaller town called Oblong. One day, my friend was reading the local wedding announcements and there was the headline—"Oblong Man Marries Normal Woman." Now the reason you are chuckling at that little joke—and countless others have enjoyed it over the past fifteen years—is because my friend remembered it and told it to me. A playful, innocent joke can multiply like loaves and fishes because one person can walk into a room and share a joke, and hundreds can leave with it!

And you can never know the full impact of sharing a joke like this or committing a "random act of comedy." A little joke and the release of laughter can change someone's day, and maybe even their lives. For eight years, my wife and I lived in a small town in Texas. For the first year or so, we had a bit of a hard time breaking the ice. One of the women who worked at the post office was not exactly unfriendly, but was certainly reserved. All that changed when I came in after Christmas one year and playfully asked what the sale price was on Christmas stamps. For some reason, this struck her as funny—and humor became a bridge between us.

Once, my wife called a local Texas boot-maker to have some boots made. When he heard her *Yankee* accent, he was decidedly aloof. Finally, he asked her, "Where you from?"

"I'm from right around here," she replied.

"No," he insisted, "I mean, where do you come from?"

When she told him she moved to Texas from Michigan, his attitude became even frostier. Then she got an idea. "Say," she said in her best Texas accent (and it was a good one), "Y'know what strikes fear into the heart of a Texan?"

"I dunno," he replied, a bit puzzled.

"A Yankee with a U-haul," she replied in a perfect Texas twangy drawl. He burst out laughing, and all of a sudden, they were friends.

Perhaps you are thinking, "I'm not a particularly funny person or a quick-thinker. How can I ever expect to come up with a clever line or joke in a tense situation?" The answer is, you don't have to. All you have to do is to have the intention of healing through humor, and the opportunities will begin to show up. After I had done my humor workshop at the beginning of a week-long retreat, one of the participants told me the following story. She was doing her laundry at the hotel, and she needed to use a dryer. Since the load in one of the dryers was already dry, she removed it and put her own clothes in. While her own clothes were drying, she decided to fold the clothes she had taken out of the dryer, even though she had no idea whose clothes they were.

She was in the middle of the folding process, when another woman burst into the laundry room. This woman was upset that there was no washer available, and began complaining loudly about people who leave their laundry unattended. She was grumpy, angry and resentful, and suddenly turned her anger on the workshop participant, "Why are you doing that person a favor and folding their laundry?" she demanded.

And in an innocent, playful voice, the workshop lady said, "What do you want me to do? Throw them on the floor?"

She said this with such humorous intent that even though it wasn't a particularly hilarious line, the grumpy woman began laughing. Her entire demeanor changed, and they began a long conversation. And when my student remarked that there was a class she wanted to attend, her new friend offered to fold her laundry for her!

The more you create a space for openhearted laughter in your life, the more you will command what the Swami calls "Farce Fields"—where the right line at the right time magically shows up. Last year, Trudy and I were eating at a favorite Chinese restaurant. All of a sudden, Trudy bit down on a hard object—a piece of steel wool in her stir-fry! Apparently, steel wool was used to clean the wok between orders, and a piece was left behind. The waiter and owner, of course, were horrified. They gave us our meals for free, and they were extremely solicitous—and very nervous— throughout the rest of our meal. Finally, the fortune cookies arrived. I sternly motioned for the waiter to come over, and I could see he was terrified. What now?
   "Excuse me," I told him, "but there's a piece of paper in my cookie."
   He exploded with laughter and the tension was released.

Ten ways to humor yourself and others

   Swami Beyondananda has said that to be happy in life, you must be able to take a joke. And if you can leave a few, all the better. Here are some ways to use healing laughter to ease your own life passages, and make life a little sweeter for others as well:
   1. *Laugh Every Day.* Seriously, laughter is good for you, especially when you choose to laugh at yourself. And when things *just aren't funny*—that's the most important time to laugh. Whenever I can, I watch *Funniest Home Videos* (I prefer it with the sound off, and some Spike Jones playing in the background) to remind me of the true nature of existence.
   2. *Practice Seeing Funny.* The idea isn't to be funny, but to learn to *see* funny. Immerse yourself in whatever kind of humor you enjoy. The more you allow humor into your life, the more you will find humor coming through you. Remember, comedy is a channel that everyone can attune to.

3. Get In the Habit of Sharing Humor. Take some of those jokes you get on the internet and share them on the *outernet*. Practice by telling the same joke to five people. Clip cartoons that you find particularly pertinent. A retiree we know puts all of his favorite comics into a scrapbook, then donates the scrapbook to a local hospital.

4. Collect Humorous Healing Stories. Jokes and funny stories are a great way to share wisdom and make a point. Keep a notebook of jokes and stories that *enlighten as they lighten*. You will find yourself remembering and using them at just the right times.

5. Turn Worry into Laughter. When you find yourself worrying about something, step back from the worry for a moment and see if you can find something in the situation to laugh about. Worrying has no proven benefits. Laughter does.

6. Reframe Suffering as Comedy in Disguise. Sing the blues when you are angry, sad or frustrated. If you must complain, complain creatively. Say, "You know what I love about this?" Look for the comedy *hidden in this picture*, (e.g., "I'm not on the verge of bankruptcy. I'm just having a near-debt experience.")

7. Build Critical Muscle by Pumping Ironies. Looking for the underlying contradictions and incongruities in situations helps develop discernment and creativity. Train your inner child to ask, "How come _____?" When you watch the news or read the papers, be on the lookout for *naked emperors*.

8. Develop a Comic Alter Ego. A shy, mild-mannered man named Edgar Bergen went *inside* and found a brash, outrageous alter ego that he called Charlie McCarthy, Together, they entertained millions—and made millions. Even if your *character* never makes it beyond your bathroom mirror, a comic alter ego is a great way to give voice to daily frustrations and lovingly laugh at your own *shadow* parts.

9. Write Your "Laugh Story." Spend an afternoon or evening writing your *life story* as if it were a comedy. Which comic actors could play your family, friends and foes? Who would you get to play your part? Give your story a title. A friend of mine calls his "Don't Do What I Did!"

10. Play Regularly. Have you ever felt the Creator is toying with you? Well then, follow the Swami's sage advice and become a creative plaything. Bring the childlike quality of play back into your life. Run up the down escalator. Dress for Halloween. Plant the seeds of harmless fun wherever you go.

Life's funny little realities

In keeping with Steve Bhaerman's sage advice, here are some thoughts to send you on your way as you begin your own mid-laugh experience.

- Blessed are those who hunger and thirst, for they are sticking to their diets.
- Life is an endless struggle full of frustrations and challenges, but eventually you find a hairstylist you like.
- You're getting old when you get the same sensation from a rocking chair that you once got from a roller coaster.
- One of the life's mysteries is how a two-pound box of candy can make a woman gain five pounds.
- It's frustrating when you know all the answers, and nobody bothers to ask you the questions.
- If you can remain calm, you just don't have all the facts.
- The real art of conversation is not only to say the right thing in the right place, but also to leave unsaid the wrong thing at the tempting moment.
- Brain cells come and brain cells go, but fat cells live forever.
- Age doesn't always bring wisdom. Sometimes age comes alone.
- You don't stop laughing because you grow old; you grow old because you stop laughing.
- Amazing! You just hang something in your closet for a while, and it shrinks two sizes.
- It is bad to suppress laughter; it goes back down and spreads to your hips.
- Age is important only if you're cheese or wine.
- The only time a woman wishes she were a year older is when she is expecting a baby.
- Freedom of the press means no-iron clothes.
- Inside some of us is a thin person struggling to get out, but she can usually be sedated with a few pieces of chocolate cake.

- Can it be a mistake that "STRESSED" is "DESSERTS" spelled backwards?
- Sometimes I think I understand everything, then I regain consciousness.

Editor's Epilogue
Martin Ducheny

Martin Ducheny is an award-winning independent writer and producer from Cincinnati, Ohio. His credits include ghost-written books and articles, executive speeches and presentations, video programs, documentaries and training seminars on personal presentation techniques. His company, Center Four Communications, Inc. can be reached at (513) 244-1700.

A reading from the book of power

What is a man doing editing a book about and for midlife women? Well, for one thing, I live with a wonderful midlife woman of power, my wife of 36 years. I have watched—and vicariously participated in—many of the ebbs and flows of the physical and emotional changes of at least one midlife woman. Still, like a man in a primitive society, I am forbidden from the women's hut and their deepest mysteries. I must look on with respect, curiosity and—yes, awe.

I believe that women hold the touchstone to remodel humanity in the coming millennium. That touchstone might be best called *the feminine*. I would call it that because this attribute is not a quality or capability unique to women or to women at any particular stage of life—although it is perhaps most realized in midlife women—and is something everyone possesses or can possess to some extent—even men. I am convinced that I see it in me, and I honor that quality and hope to nurture it.

Although *the feminine* is not the exclusive territory of women, culturally they are closer to it. They also have the economic, political, artistic, emotional and spiritual power to press forward. This power is generally strongest in midlife women although, again, this is not exclusively their territory.

Phenomenal Women: That's Us! was conceived to vitalize the power of *the feminine* in women who would like to make this journey. From this power in action will flow the further awakening to their essential nature and their strength to further the agenda of the Mother Earth by being most fully feminine. As I see it, this is a joyful task, a heavy burden borne lightly, a celebration of sisterhood that will draw *the masculine* world along with it.

This book is a marvelous collection of ideas and techniques that stands before you now as the seed crystal, the inspiration for such a change. It is valuable and thought provoking. If taken to heart by enough women, perhaps it could even change the structure of society.

Still the question, "Why a man to edit a book for women?" The answer is, of course—because we are *all* in this together.

The Eastern *yin-yang* symbol shows what I mean. The mysterious female *yin* is balanced by the blatant male *yang*, but both are complementarily intertwined. In the center of each half is a burning dot of the opposite soul energy, indicating that each individual must also balance *yin* and *yang* within her or himself. Together and in balance, *yin* and *yang* make a perfect circle—harmony.

Many women have spent their lives doing what comes naturally under an old paradigm. When it was time to attract mates, they attracted a mate. When it was time to bear children, they bore children. When it was time to make a nest-like home, they made a home. They encouraged and supported their mates toward greater and greater economic power and enjoyed sharing the glow of success. Now, as they enter midlife, women can find themselves more powerful than ever.

This book offers techniques, motivation and encouragement to constantly keep their physical, emotional and spiritual batteries charged. This super-charging is a first step on the way to generating the energy of a *new paradigm of power* for women—and a new balance of *the masculine* and *the feminine* in society. Attend to what *Phenomenal Women* has to say, and if a muse calls to you from its pages, follow her. Fully charged and feeling *powerful*, take your next step into the future.

> In the words of John Wesley:
> "Do all the good you can,
> In all the ways you can,
> In all the places you can,
> To all the people you can,
> As long as you ever can."

About the Author

By helping others help themselves, Dr. Madeleine Singer has come full circle in her own search for the ultimate self. Her philosophy of Changing Ordinary to Extraordinary has served to make her a dynamic and effective educator for personal productivity and performance. Globally, she currently works with Fortune 500 Corporations, universities, professional athletes, and groups of all sizes in the areas of creative thinking, stress management, productivity and effectiveness training, including relaxation techniques for transformational growth.

Born in New York and raised in Connecticut, she received her B.S. in Education with majors in science and psychology. Dr. Singer is certified in Therapeutic Touch by New York University School of Nursing and in Psychic Development by the Patricia Hayes School of Inner Sense Development. Her extensive training includes herbology, nutrition, acupressure and myotherapy, and she is experienced in Time Line Development. Dr. Singer is a practitioner of Neuro-Linguistic Programming with majors in education, health, creativity and leadership. She also has attained her Doctorate in Clinical Hypnotherapy.

Madeleine has produced and hosted two television series, "The Holistic Approach" and "Energetix." She is a life enrichment columnist for several magazines and the author of three other books, *Insights*; *The Psychology of Synergy*; and *Power Up For Success* (all New Falcon Publications).

ALSO FROM DR. MADELEINE SINGER

INSIGHTS

Introduced by Timothy Leary, Ph.D.

"... change for growth becomes fun and easy with Maddy's techniques."
— Director, Balance Center, Branford, CT

"Charismatic and exciting... People want to better their lives and Madeleine gives the techniques to do so."
— Midday Club, Stamford, CT

"An unusual, courageous, playful book. A Tao Te Ching for the New Age. Accessible. Inviting. Guaranteed to raise a smile."
— Timothy Leary, Ph.D. author of *Info-Psychology*

ISBN 0-941404-94-3

ALSO FROM DR. MADELEINE SINGER

POWER UP FOR SUCCESS

"Maddy answers questions of relaxed living, dealing with one's anxieties, and helps each reader to cope with understanding the hidden meanings of our own lives. I highly recommend this book for peace of mind, tranquility, and longevity with happiness. Bravo!"
— Joseph Waxberg, M.D., Psychiatrist

"Maddy and vitamins — a daily dose of both enhances health."
— John Conners, Global Broadcasting, Inc.

ISBN 1-56184-070-X

ALSO FROM DR. MADELEINE SINGER

THE PSYCHOLOGY OF SYNERGY
A Guide To Personal Power
Introduced by Robert Anton Wilson, Ph.D.

"Maddy's done the hard work for us, sifting through the fool's gold to find the real nuggets."
— Lynn Schroeder, Superlearning Institute

"Maddy is a living, breathing example of what works."
— Frank Gerardi, President, Univest Management, Inc.

Maddy's healing energy is contagious…"
— Vincent Valles, Mayer Medical Center

ISBN 0-941404-03-X